# Fantastic Four

## ALL FOR ONE

STAR
BO-ZU

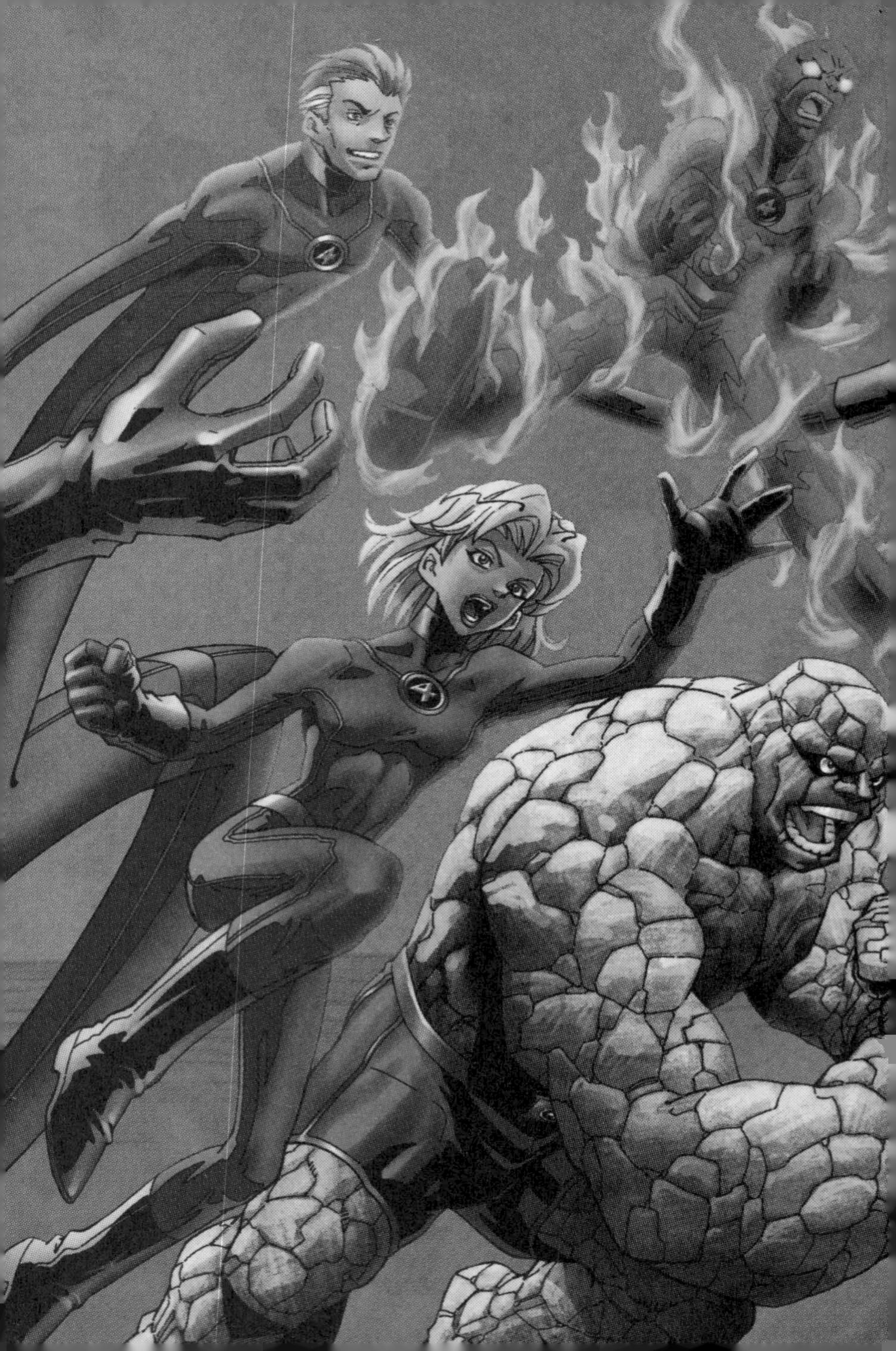

# Fantastic Four
## Four
### ALL FOR ONE

Writer: Sean McKeever

Art: Makoto Nakatsuka, Gurihiru, Joe Dodd with
Derek Fridolfs, & Alitha Martinez with David Newbold

Colors: SotoColors

Letters: Dave Sharpe

Special Thanks to: Mitsuko Mitsuoka

Assistant Editor: MacKenzie Cadenhead

Editor: C.B. Cebulski

Consulting Editor: Ralph Macchio

Collections Editor: Jeff Youngquist

Assistant Editor: Jennifer Grünwald

Book Designer: Carrie Beadle

Editor in Chief: Joe Quesada

Publisher: Dan Buckley

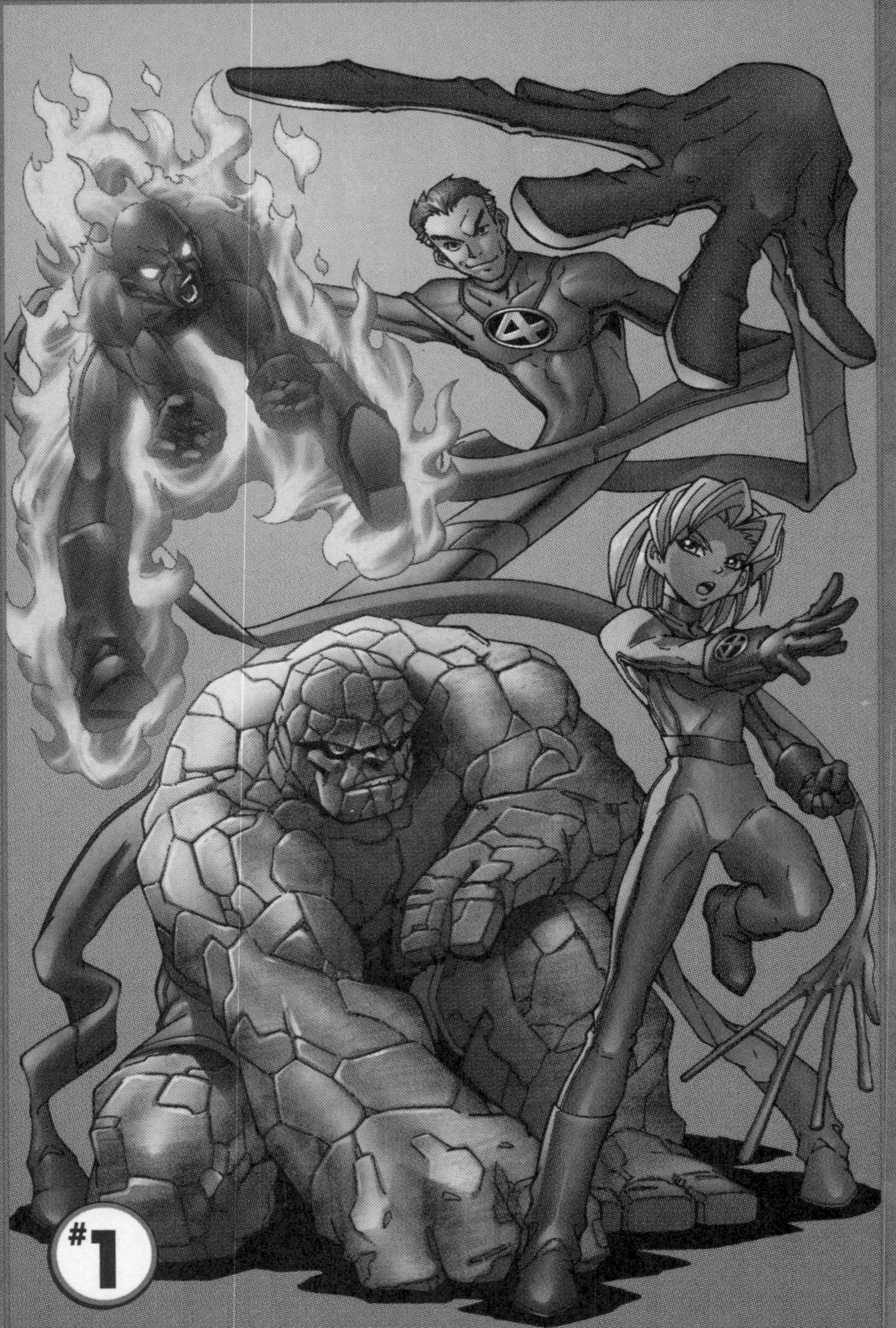
#1

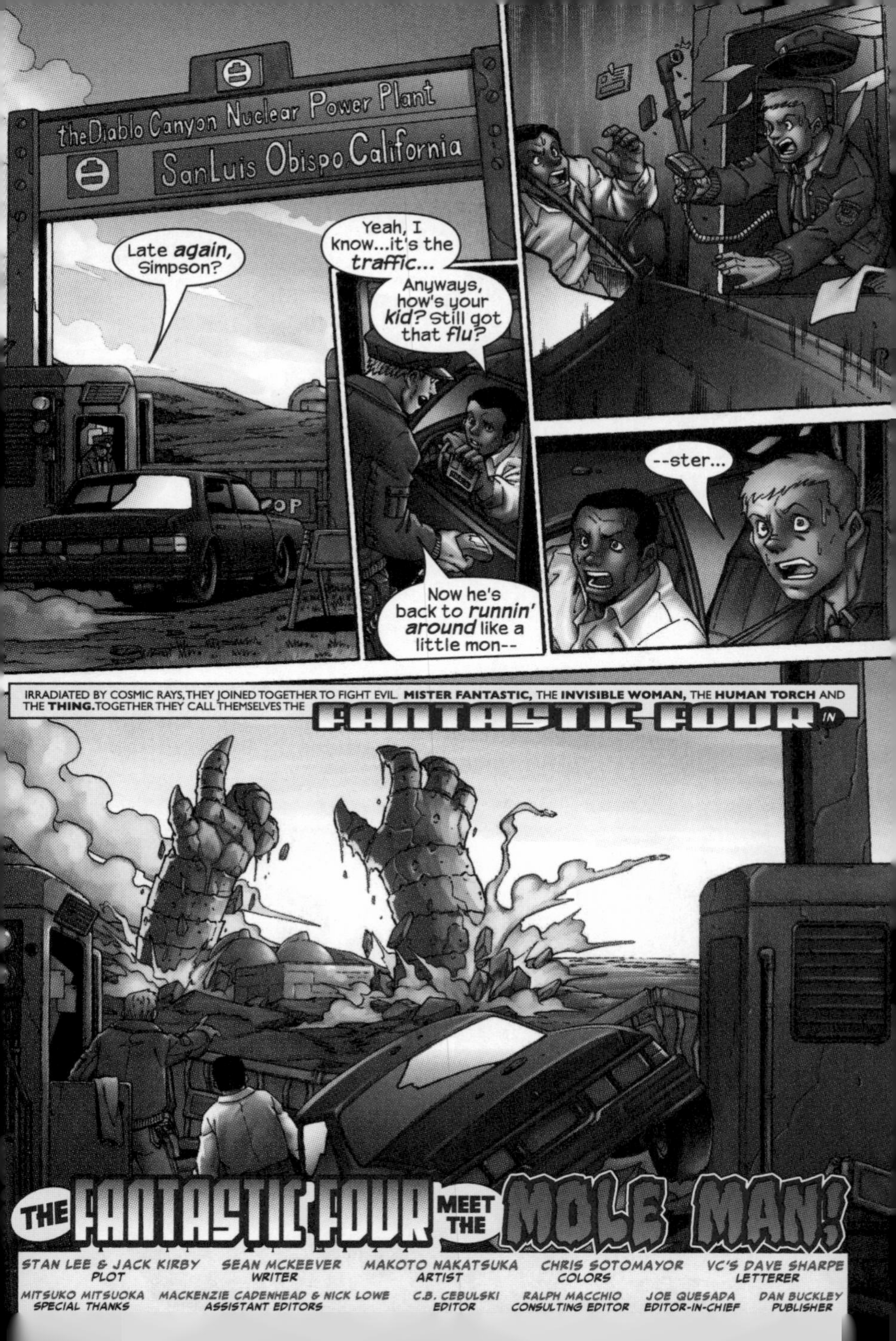
the Diablo Canyon Nuclear Power Plant
San Luis Obispo, California
Late again, Simpson?
Yeah, I know...it's the traffic...
Anyways, how's your kid? Still got that flu?
Now he's back to runnin' around like a little mon--
--ster...
IRRADIATED BY COSMIC RAYS, THEY JOINED TOGETHER TO FIGHT EVIL. MISTER FANTASTIC, THE INVISIBLE WOMAN, THE HUMAN TORCH AND THE THING. TOGETHER THEY CALL THEMSELVES THE FANTASTIC FOUR IN
THE FANTASTIC FOUR MEET THE MOLE MAN!
STAN LEE & JACK KIRBY PLOT
SEAN MCKEEVER WRITER
MAKOTO NAKATSUKA ARTIST
CHRIS SOTOMAYOR COLORS
VC'S DAVE SHARPE LETTERER
MITSUKO MITSUOKA SPECIAL THANKS
MACKENZIE CADENHEAD & NICK LOWE ASSISTANT EDITORS
C.B. CEBULSKI EDITOR
RALPH MACCHIO CONSULTING EDITOR
JOE QUESADA EDITOR-IN-CHIEF
DAN BUCKLEY PUBLISHER

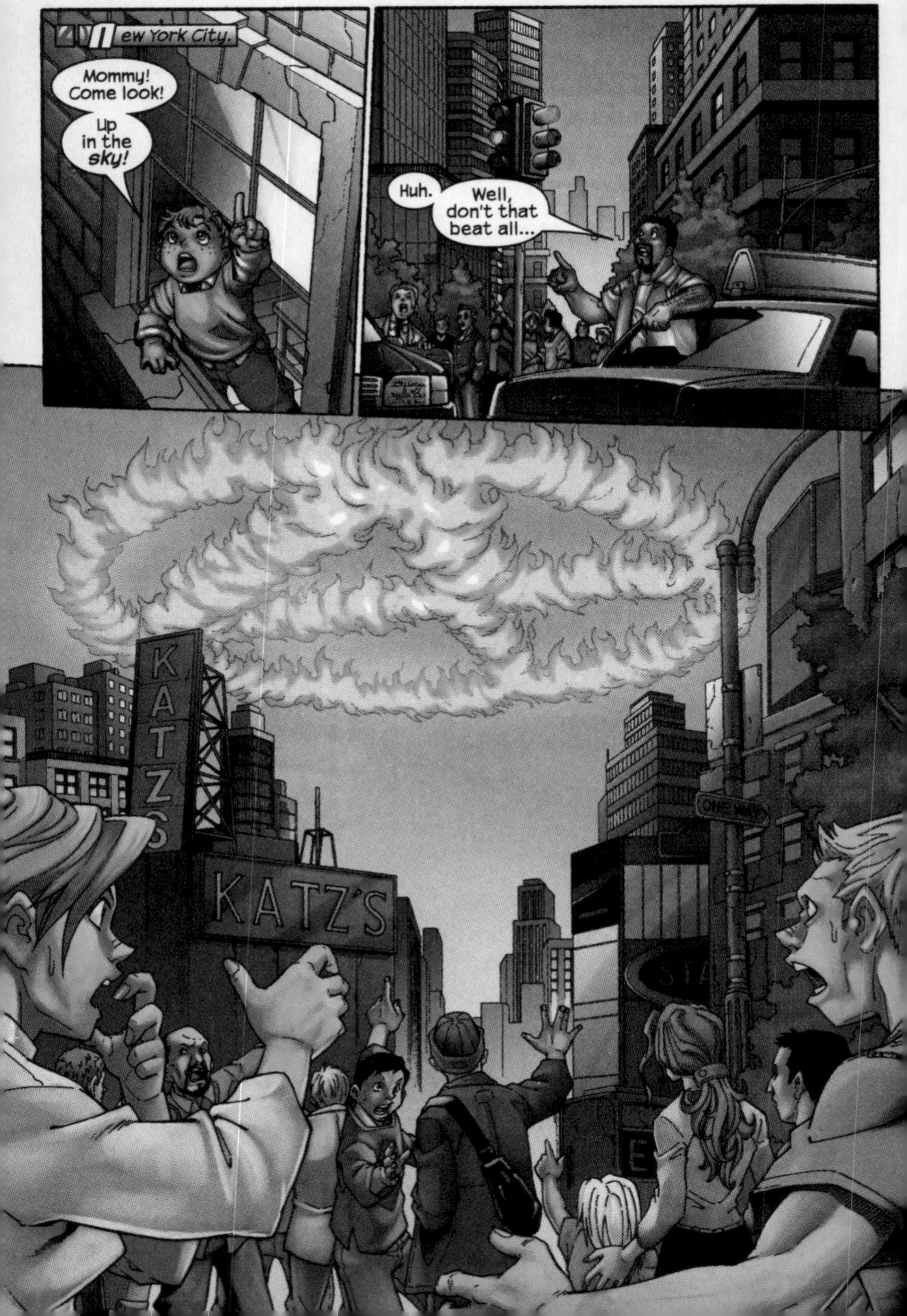
New York City.
Mommy! Come look!
Up in the sky!
Huh.
Well, don't that beat all...
KATZ'S
KATZ'S
ONE WAY

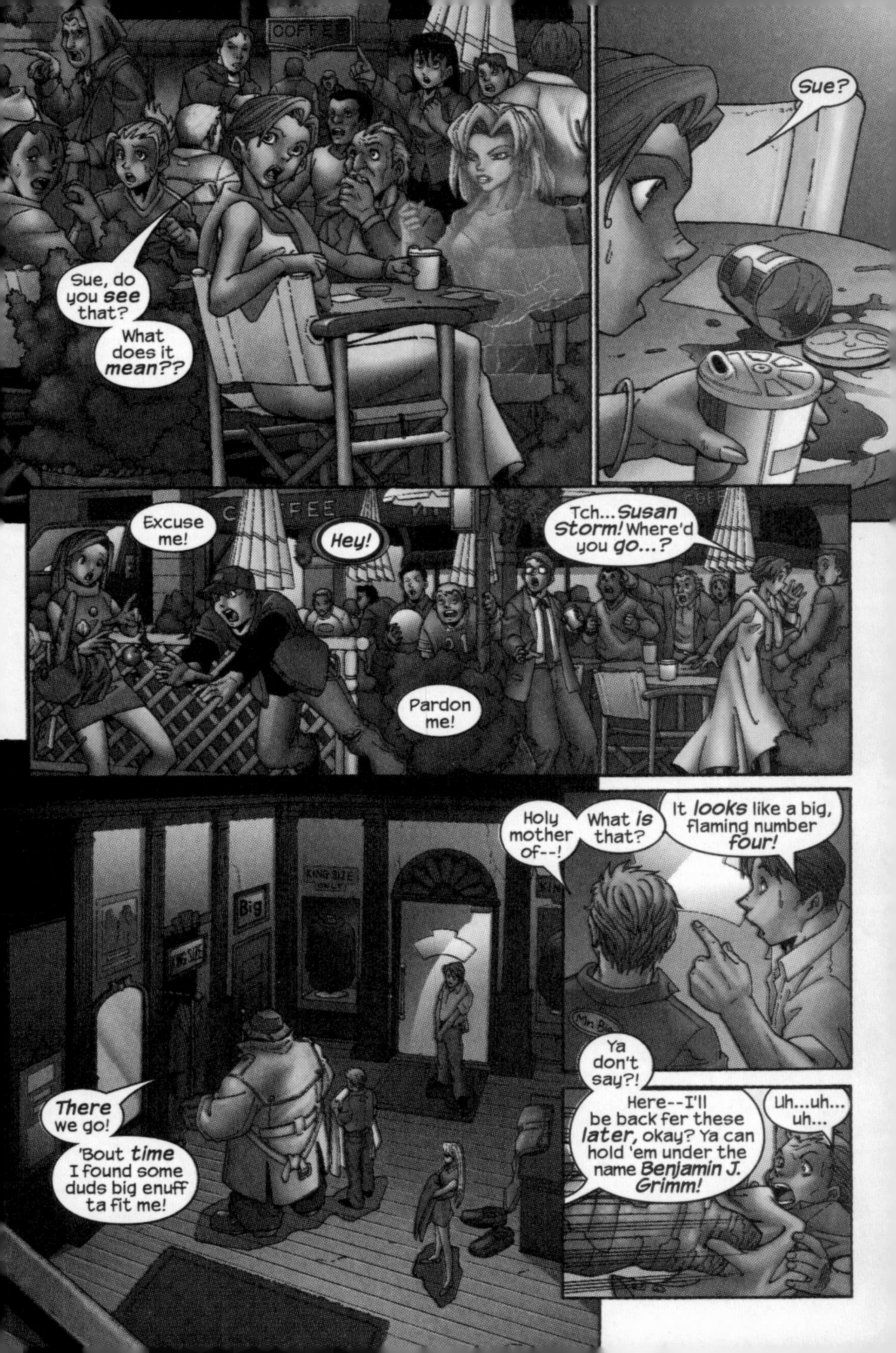
Sue, do you see that?
What does it mean??
Sue?
Excuse me!
Hey!
Tch... Susan Storm! Where'd you go...?
Pardon me!
Holy mother of--!
What is that?
It looks like a big, flaming number four!
Ya don't say?!
Here--I'll be back fer these later, okay? Ya can hold 'em under the name Benjamin J. Grimm!
Uh...uh... uh...
There we go!
'Bout time I found some duds big enuff ta fit me!
COFFEE
KING SIZE ONLY
Big
KING SIZE

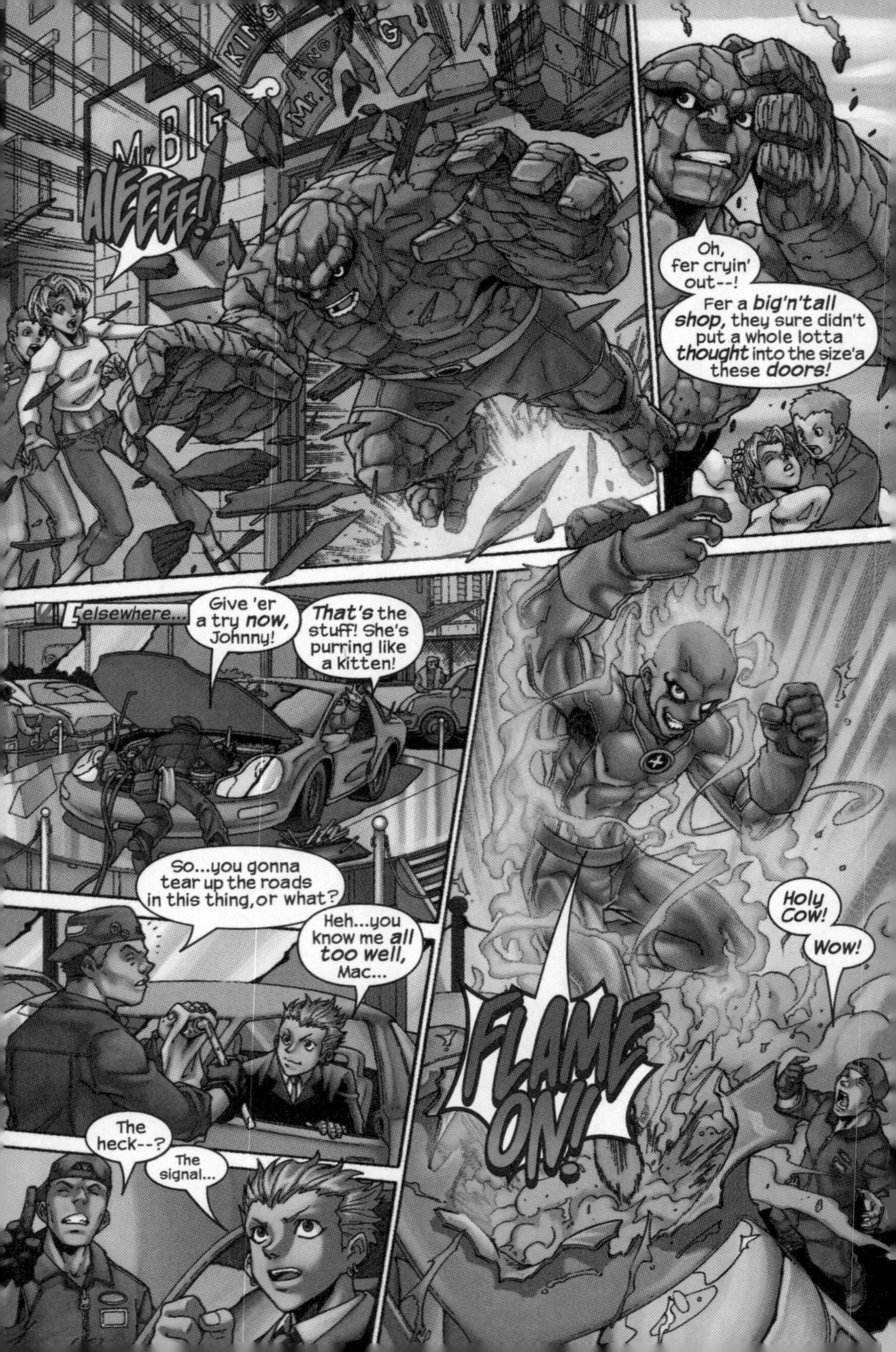

Mr BIG
KING
AIEEEE!
Oh, fer cryin' out--!
Fer a big'n'tall shop, they sure didn't put a whole lotta thought into the size'a these doors!
Elsewhere...
Give 'er a try now, Johnny!
That's the stuff! She's purring like a kitten!
So...you gonna tear up the roads in this thing,or what?
Heh...you know me all too well, Mac...
The heck--?
The signal...
FLAME ON!
Holy Cow!
Wow!

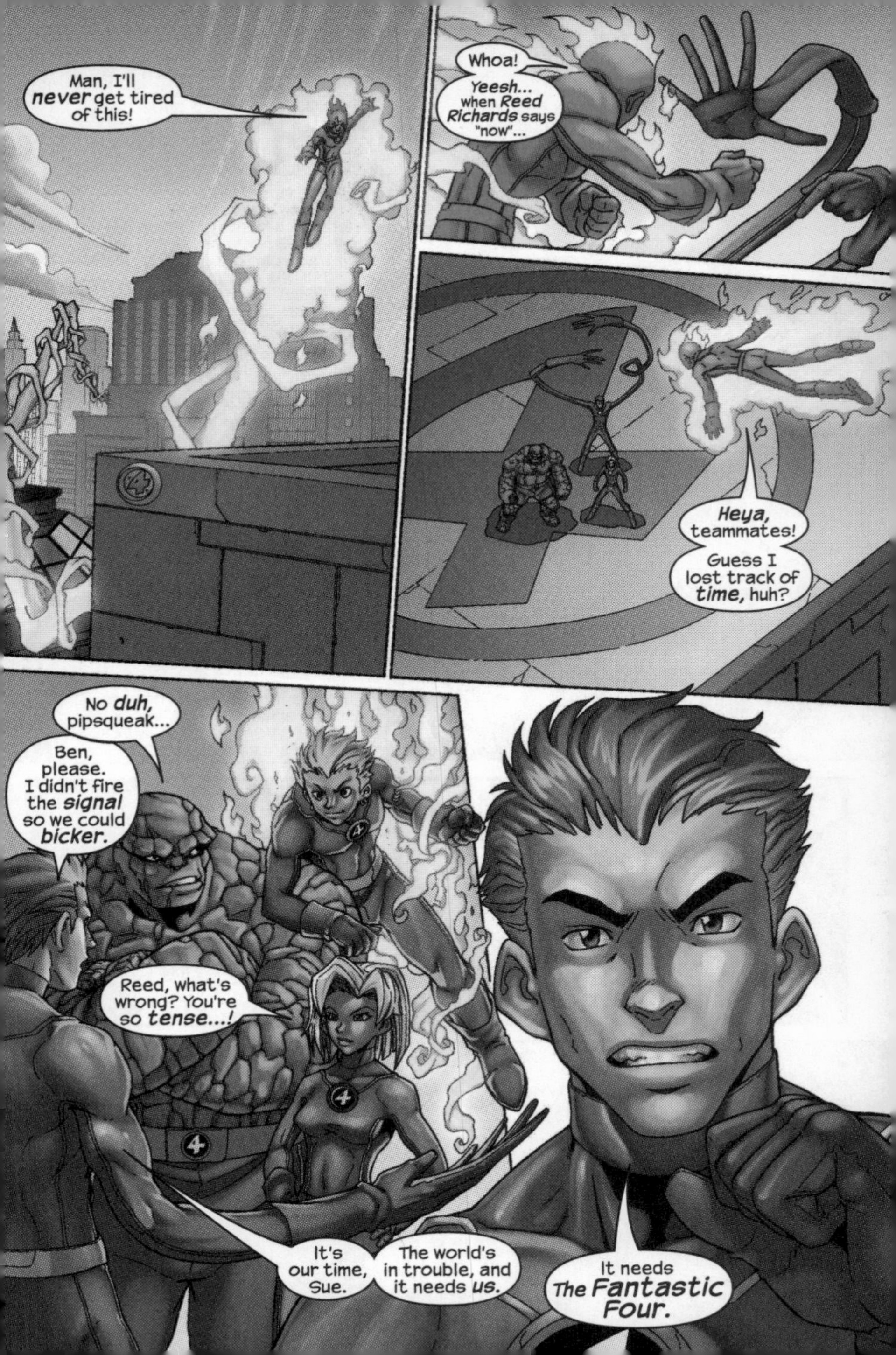
Man, I'll *never* get tired of this!
Whoa!
*Yeesh...* when *Reed Richards* says "now"...
*Heya,* teammates!
Guess I lost track of *time,* huh?
No *duh,* pipsqueak...
Ben, please. I didn't fire the *signal* so we could *bicker.*
Reed, what's wrong? You're so *tense...!*
It's our time, Sue.
The world's in trouble, and it needs *us.*
It needs *The Fantastic Four.*

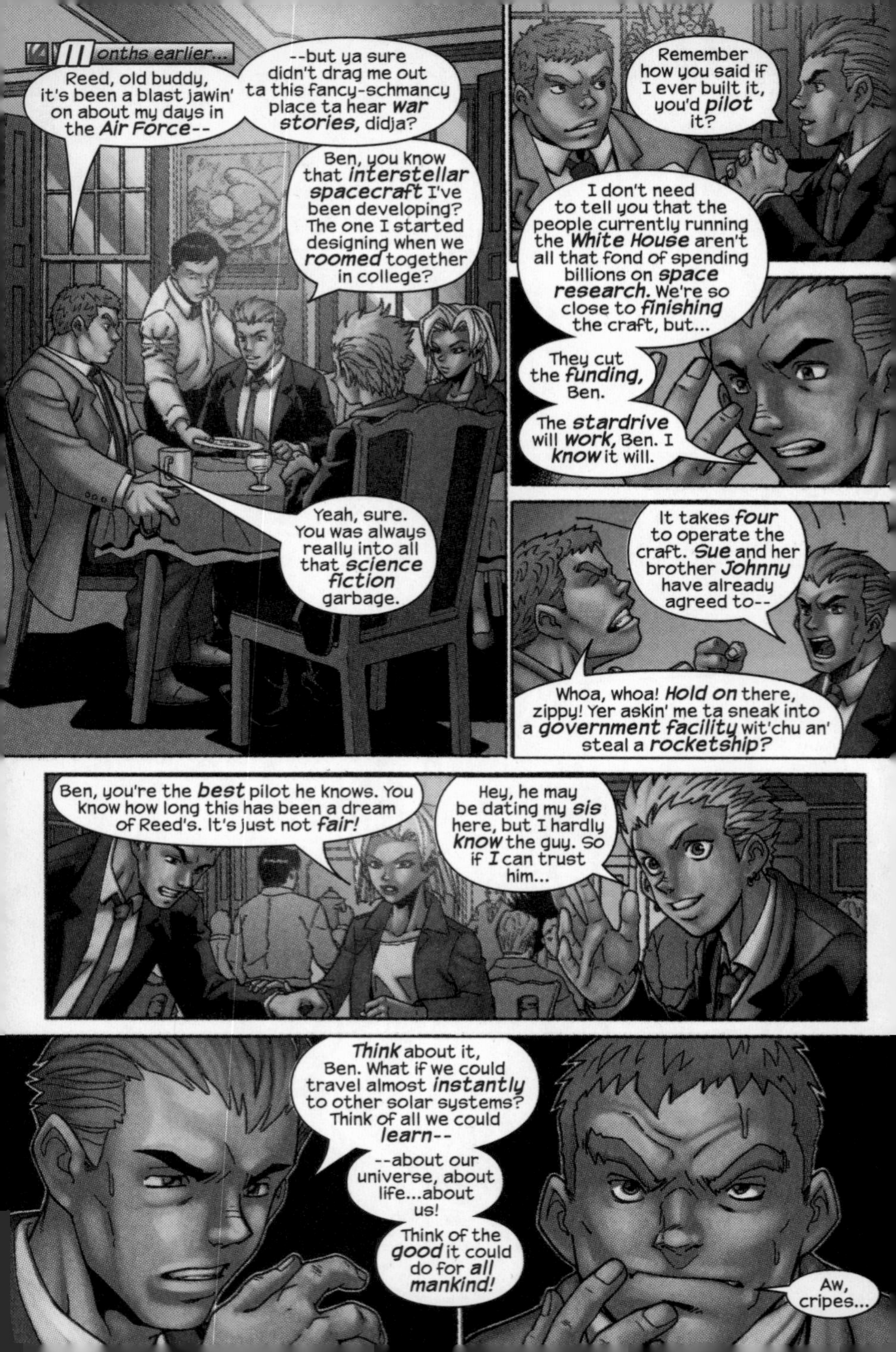
Months earlier...
Reed, old buddy, it's been a blast jawin' on about my days in the Air Force--
--but ya sure didn't drag me out ta this fancy-schmancy place ta hear war stories, didja?
Ben, you know that interstellar spacecraft I've been developing? The one I started designing when we roomed together in college?
Yeah, sure. You was always really into all that science fiction garbage.
Remember how you said if I ever built it, you'd pilot it?
I don't need to tell you that the people currently running the White House aren't all that fond of spending billions on space research. We're so close to finishing the craft, but...
They cut the funding, Ben.
The stardrive will work, Ben. I know it will.
It takes four to operate the craft. Sue and her brother Johnny have already agreed to--
Whoa, whoa! Hold on there, zippy! Yer askin' me ta sneak into a government facility wit'chu an' steal a rocketship?
Ben, you're the best pilot he knows. You know how long this has been a dream of Reed's. It's just not fair!
Hey, he may be dating my sis here, but I hardly know the guy. So if I can trust him...
Think about it, Ben. What if we could travel almost instantly to other solar systems? Think of all we could learn--
--about our universe, about life...about us!
Think of the good it could do for all mankind!
Aw, cripes...

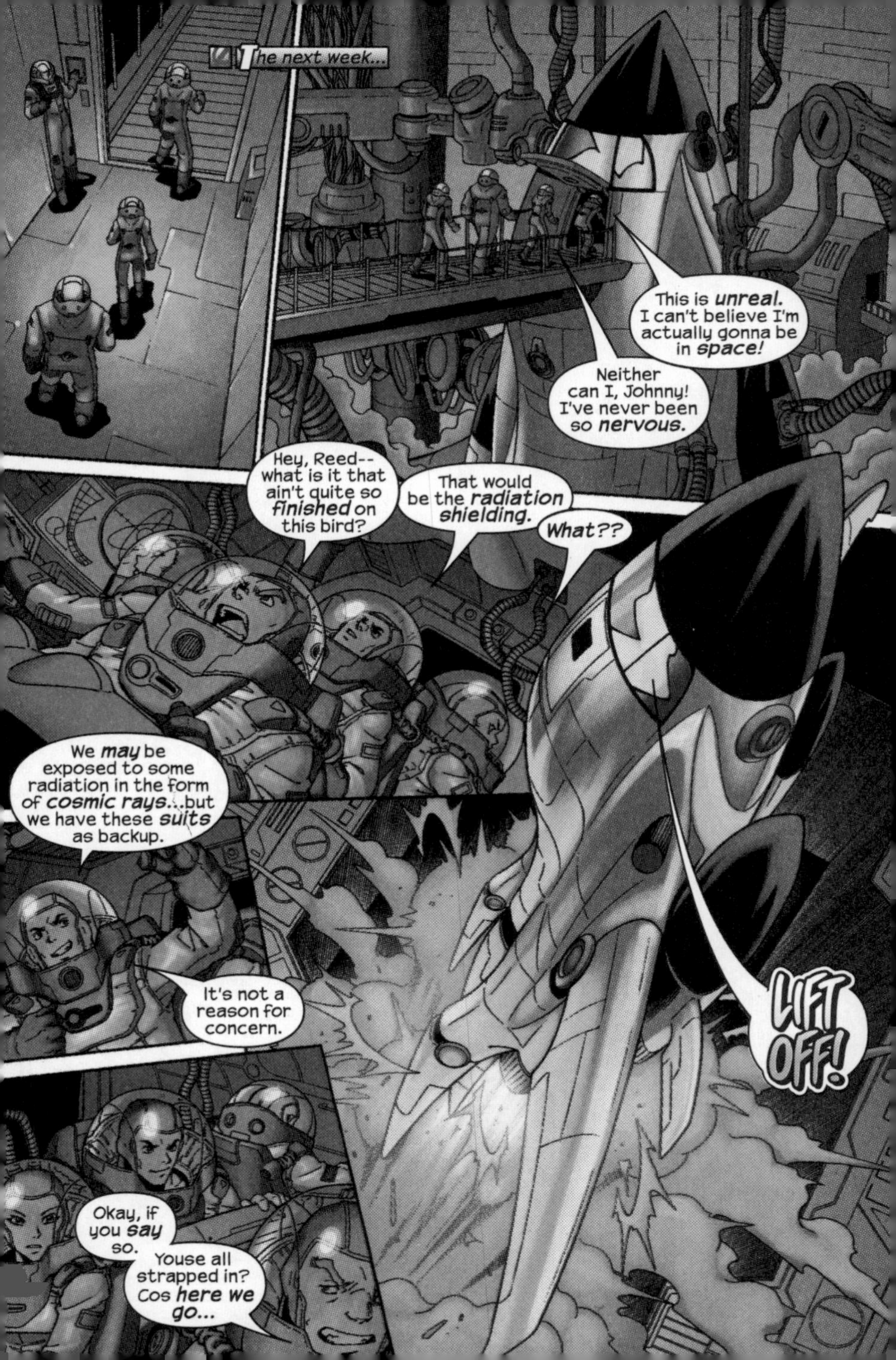
The next week...
This is *unreal.* I can't believe I'm actually gonna be in *space!*
Neither can I, Johnny! I've never been so *nervous.*
Hey, Reed-- what is it that ain't quite so *finished* on this bird?
That would be the *radiation shielding.*
*What??*
We *may* be exposed to some radiation in the form of *cosmic rays*...but we have these *suits* as backup.
It's not a reason for concern.
LIFT OFF!
Okay, if you *say* so.
Youse all strapped in? Cos *here we go...*

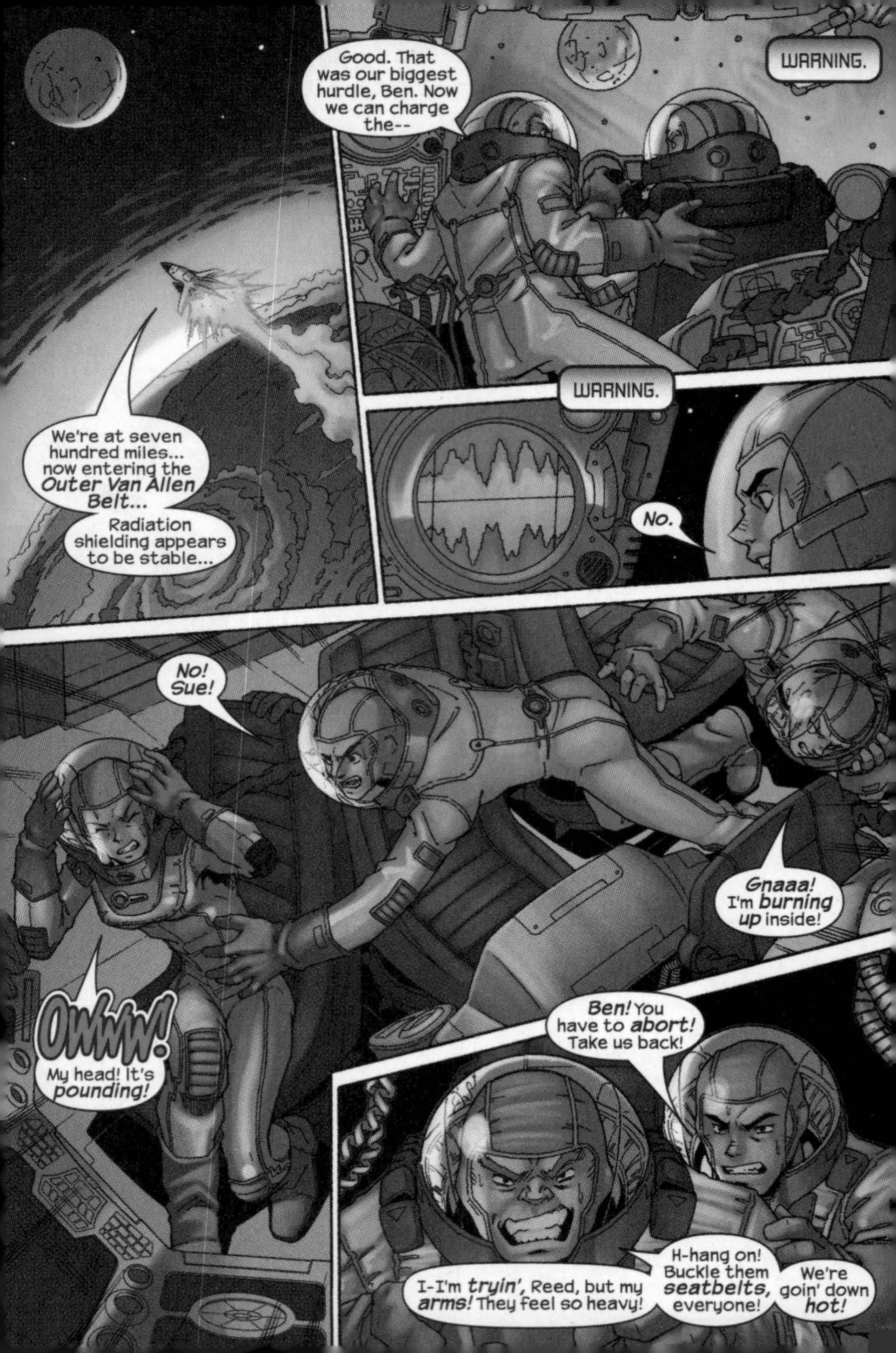
We're at seven hundred miles... now entering the *Outer Van Allen Belt*...
Radiation shielding appears to be stable...
Good. That was our biggest hurdle, Ben. Now we can charge the--
WARNING.
WARNING.
No.
No! Sue!
Gnaaa! I'm *burning up* inside!
OWWW!
My head! It's *pounding!*
*Ben!* You have to *abort!* Take us back!
I-I'm *tryin'*, Reed, but my *arms!* They feel so heavy!
H-hang on! Buckle them *seatbelts,* everyone!
We're goin' down *hot!*

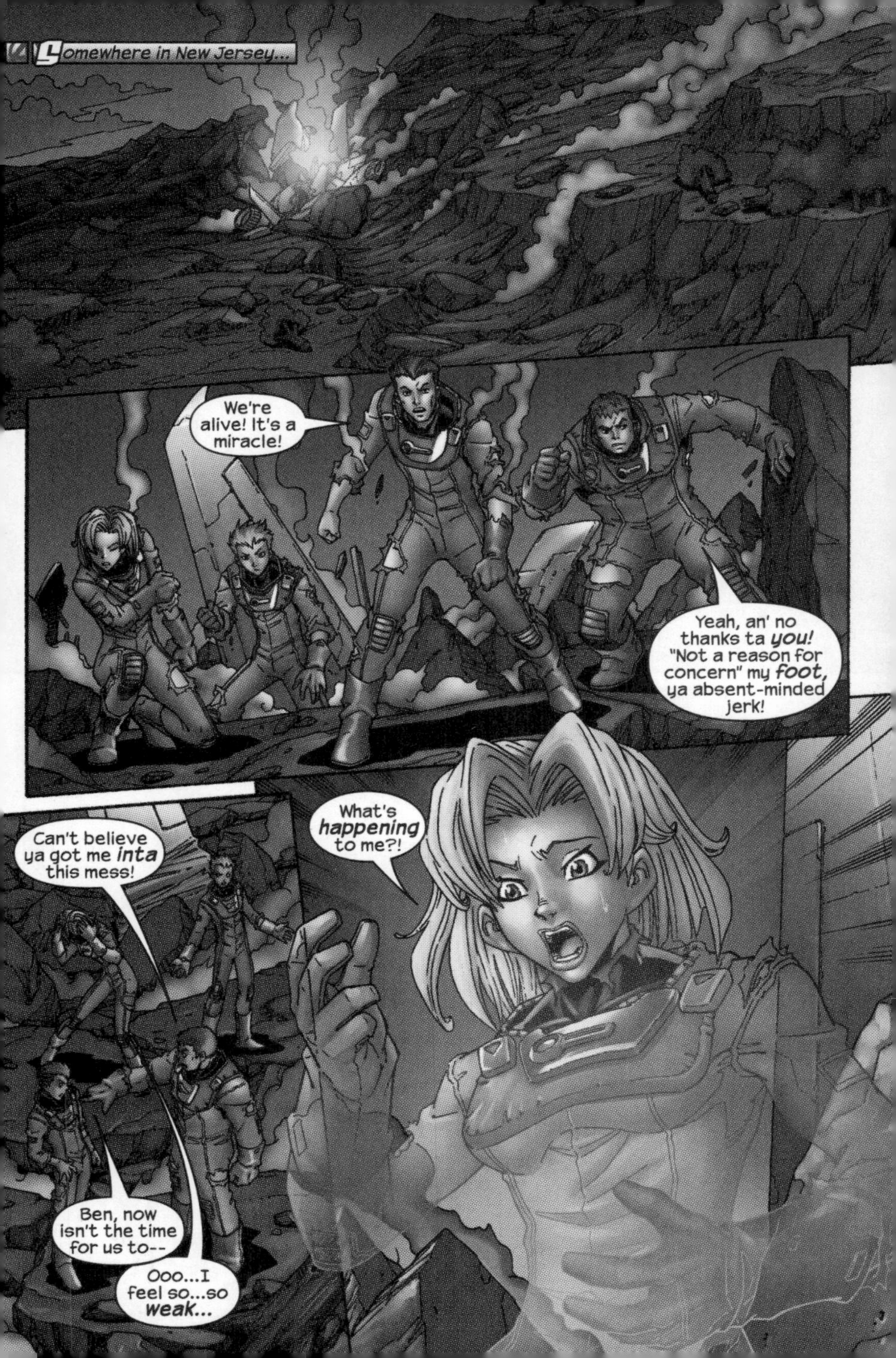
Somewhere in New Jersey...
We're alive! It's a miracle!
Yeah, an' no thanks ta you! "Not a reason for concern" my foot, ya absent-minded jerk!
Can't believe ya got me inta this mess!
What's happening to me?!
Ben, now isn't the time for us to--
Ooo...I feel so...so weak...

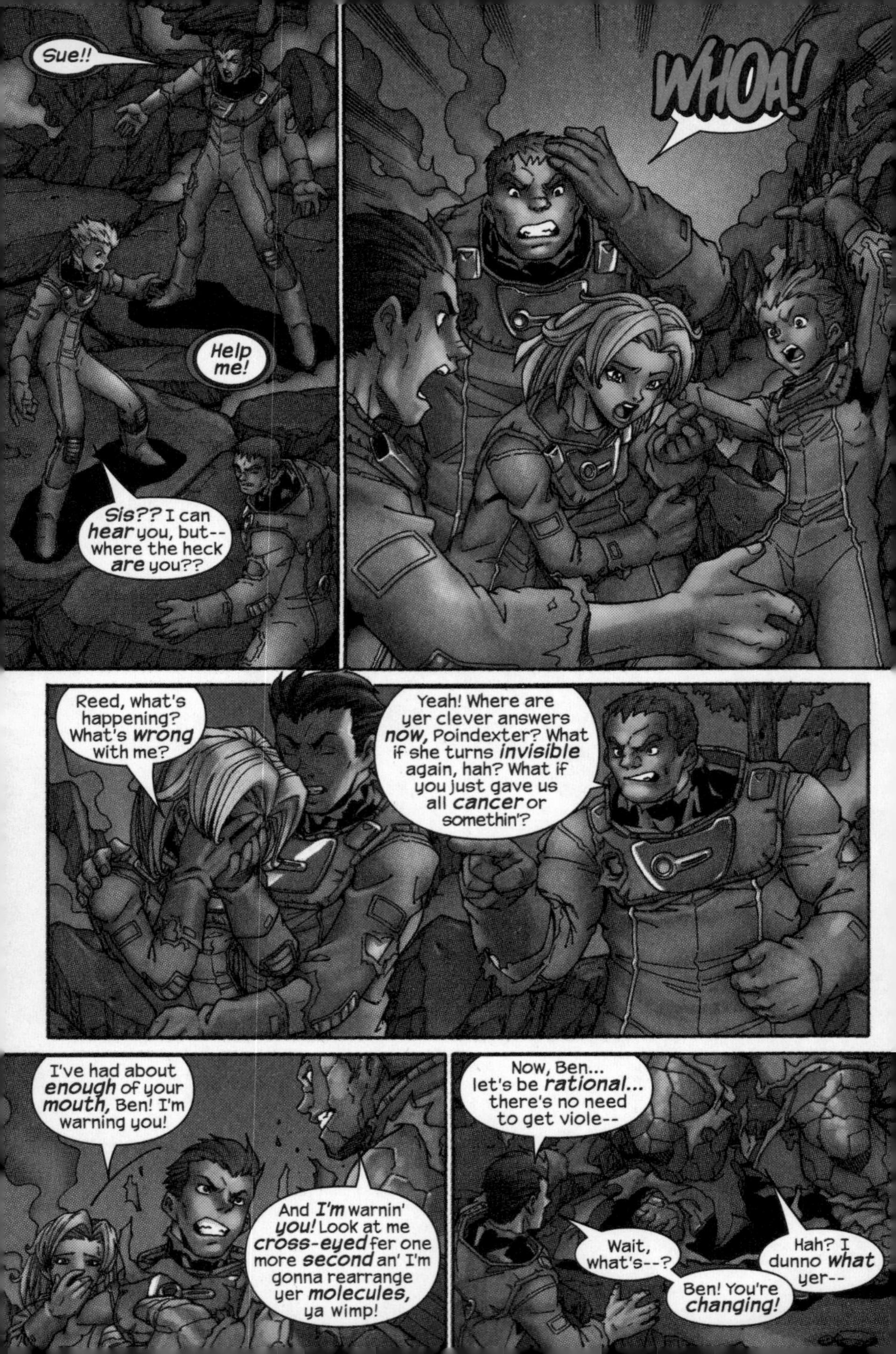
Sue!!
Help me!
Sis?? I can hear you, but-- where the heck are you??
WHOA!
Reed, what's happening? What's wrong with me?
Yeah! Where are yer clever answers now, Poindexter? What if she turns invisible again, hah? What if you just gave us all cancer or somethin'?
I've had about enough of your mouth, Ben! I'm warning you!
And I'm warnin' you! Look at me cross-eyed fer one more second an' I'm gonna rearrange yer molecules, ya wimp!
Now, Ben... let's be rational... there's no need to get viole--
Wait, what's--?
Hah? I dunno what yer--
Ben! You're changing!

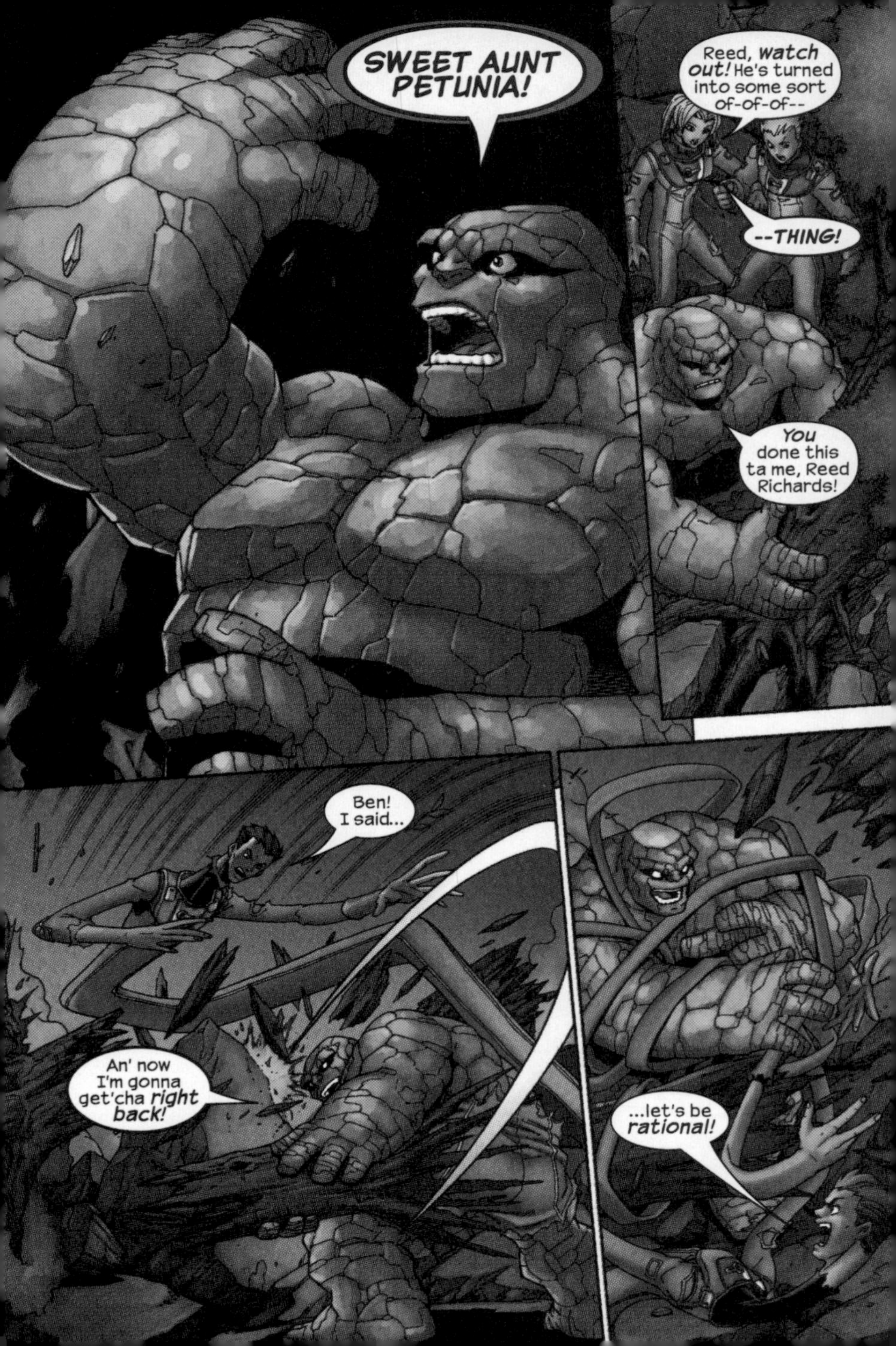
SWEET AUNT PETUNIA!
Reed, watch out! He's turned into some sort of-of-of--
--THING!
You done this ta me, Reed Richards!
Ben! I said...
An' now I'm gonna get'cha right back!
...let's be rational!

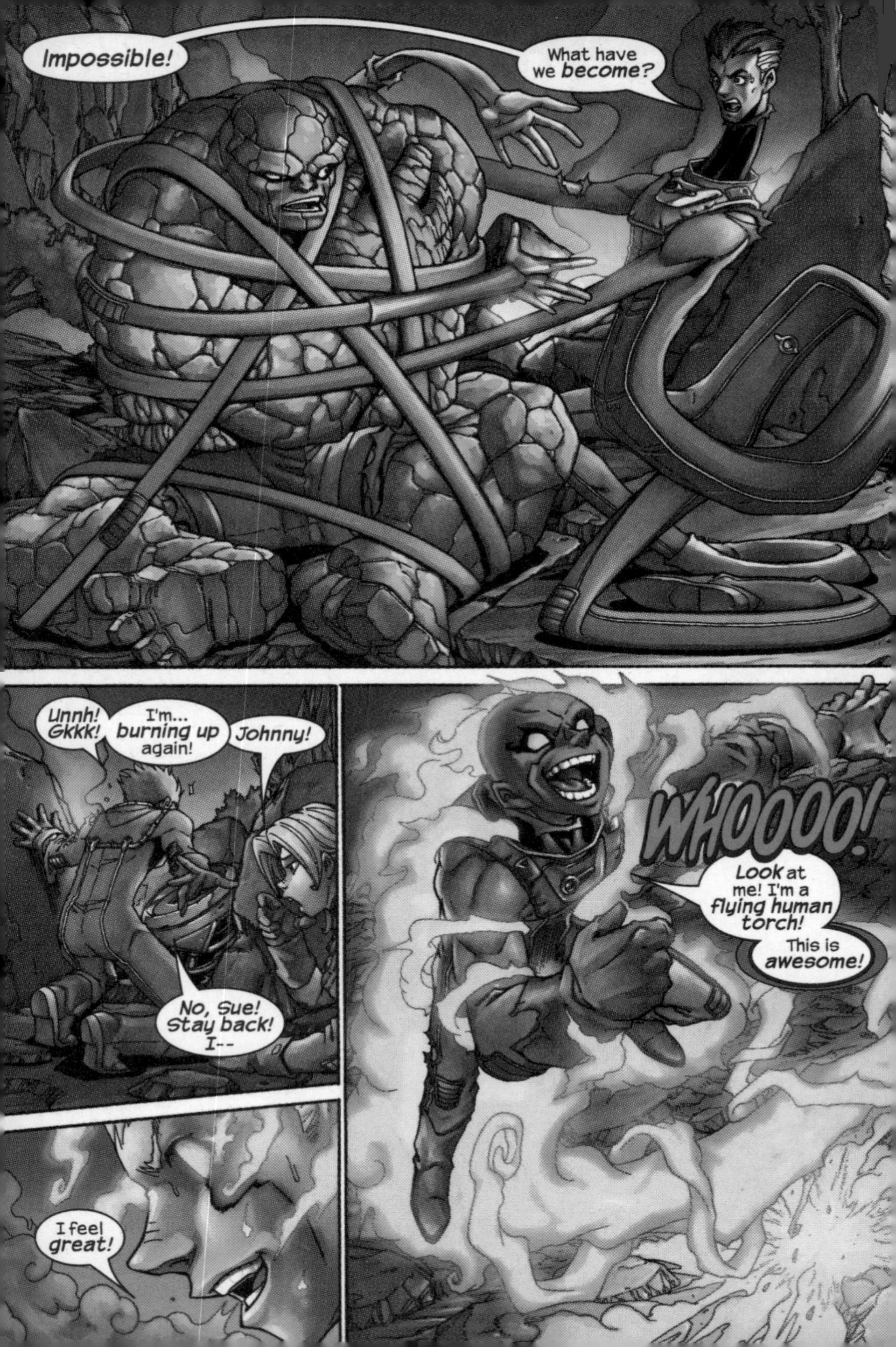
Impossible!
What have we become?
Unnh! Gkkk!
I'm... burning up again!
Johnny!
No, Sue! Stay back! I--
I feel great!
WHOOOO!
Look at me! I'm a flying human torch!
This is awesome!

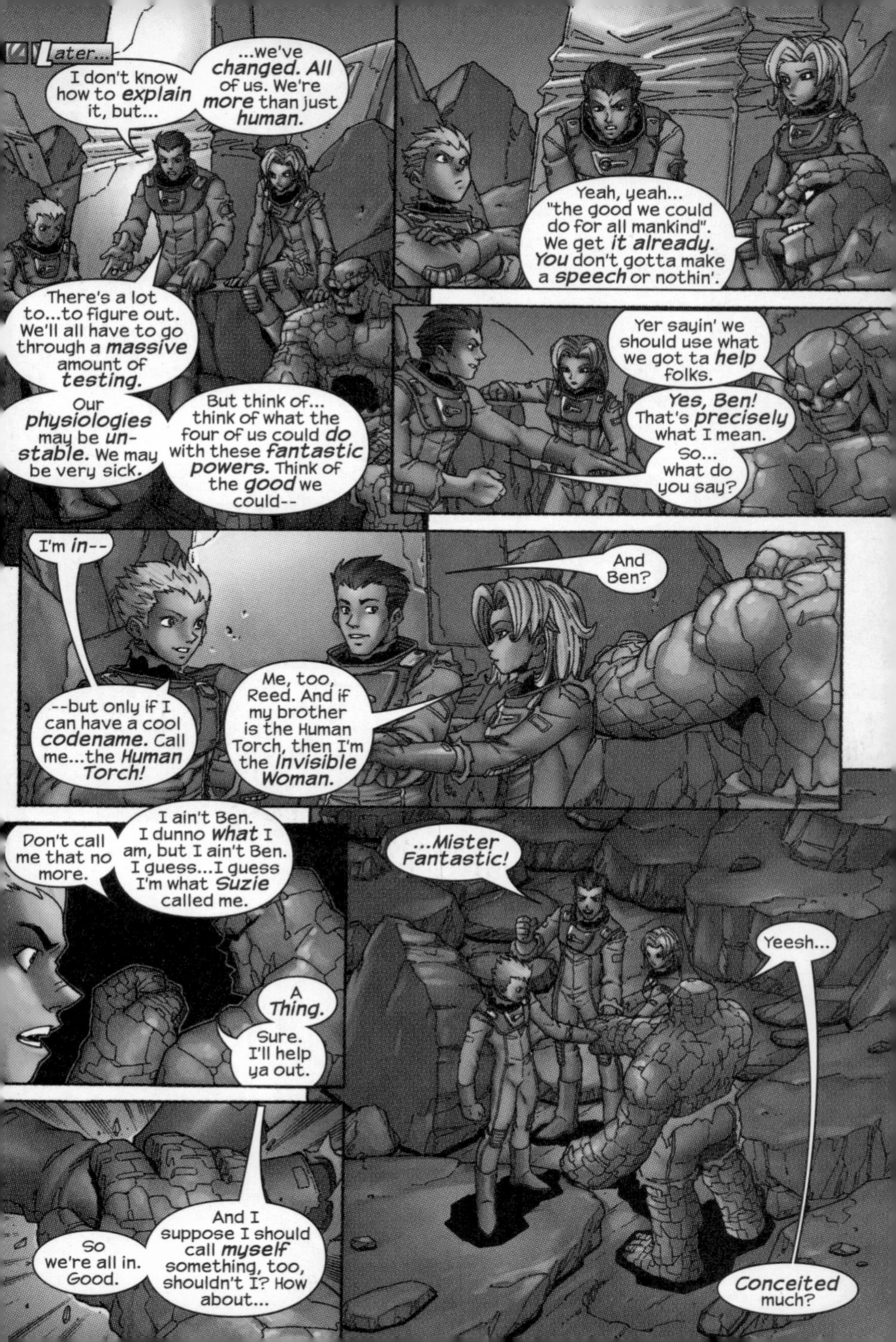
Later...
I don't know how to explain it, but...
...we've changed. All of us. We're more than just human.
There's a lot to...to figure out. We'll all have to go through a massive amount of testing.
Our physiologies may be unstable. We may be very sick.
But think of... think of what the four of us could do with these fantastic powers. Think of the good we could--
Yeah, yeah... "the good we could do for all mankind". We get it already. You don't gotta make a speech or nothin'.
Yer sayin' we should use what we got ta help folks.
Yes, Ben! That's precisely what I mean.
So... what do you say?
I'm in--
--but only if I can have a cool codename. Call me...the Human Torch!
Me, too, Reed. And if my brother is the Human Torch, then I'm the Invisible Woman.
And Ben?
Don't call me that no more.
I ain't Ben. I dunno what I am, but I ain't Ben. I guess...I guess I'm what Suzie called me.
A Thing.
Sure. I'll help ya out.
So we're all in. Good.
And I suppose I should call myself something, too, shouldn't I? How about...
...Mister Fantastic!
Yeesh...
Conceited much?

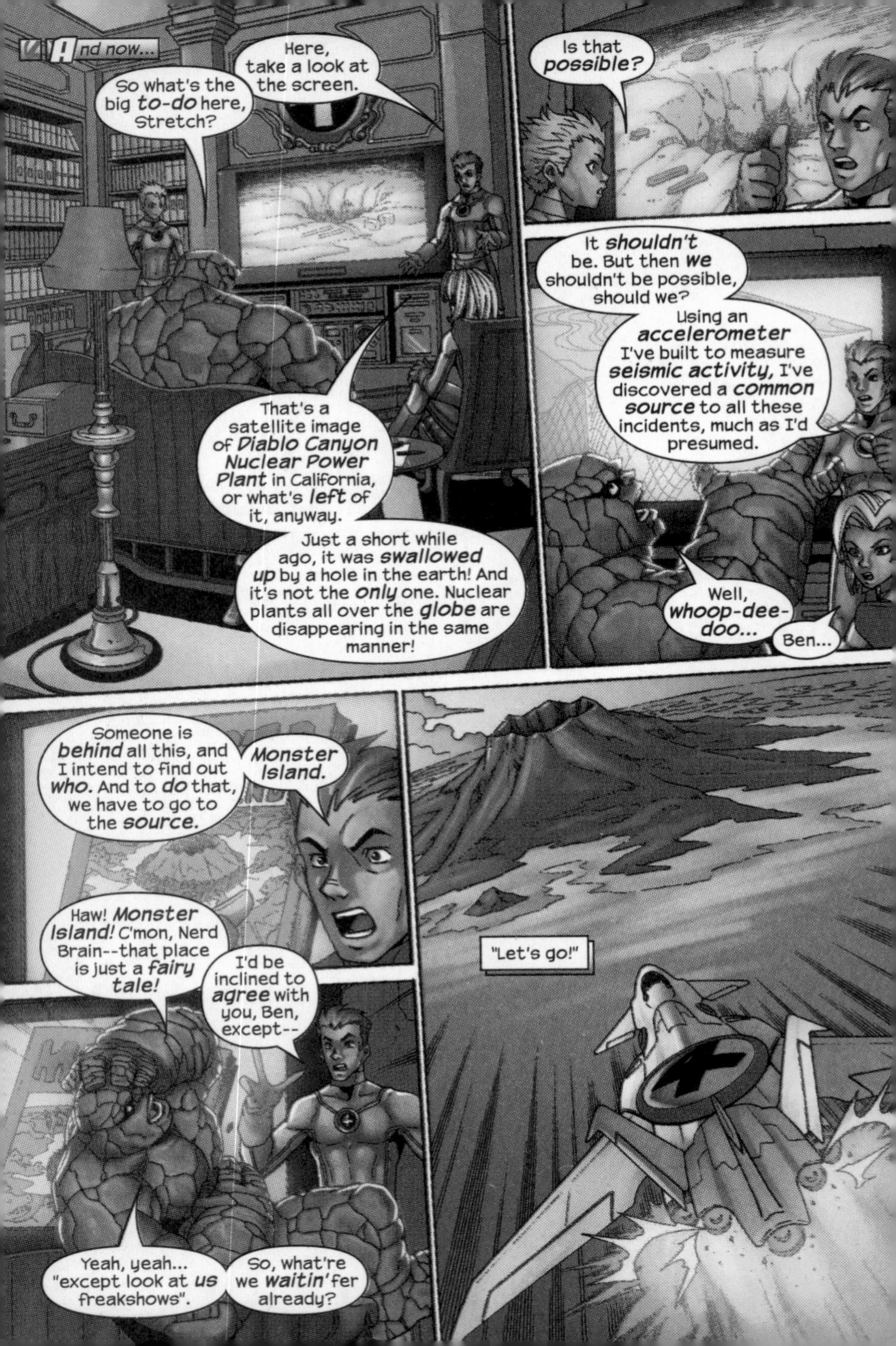
And now...
So what's the big to-do here, Stretch?
Here, take a look at the screen.
That's a satellite image of Diablo Canyon Nuclear Power Plant in California, or what's left of it, anyway.
Just a short while ago, it was swallowed up by a hole in the earth! And it's not the only one. Nuclear plants all over the globe are disappearing in the same manner!
Is that possible?
It shouldn't be. But then we shouldn't be possible, should we?
Using an accelerometer I've built to measure seismic activity, I've discovered a common source to all these incidents, much as I'd presumed.
Well, whoop-dee-doo...
Ben...
Someone is behind all this, and I intend to find out who. And to do that, we have to go to the source.
Monster Island.
Haw! Monster Island! C'mon, Nerd Brain--that place is just a fairy tale!
I'd be inclined to agree with you, Ben, except--
Yeah, yeah... "except look at us freakshows".
So, what're we waitin' fer already?
"Let's go!"

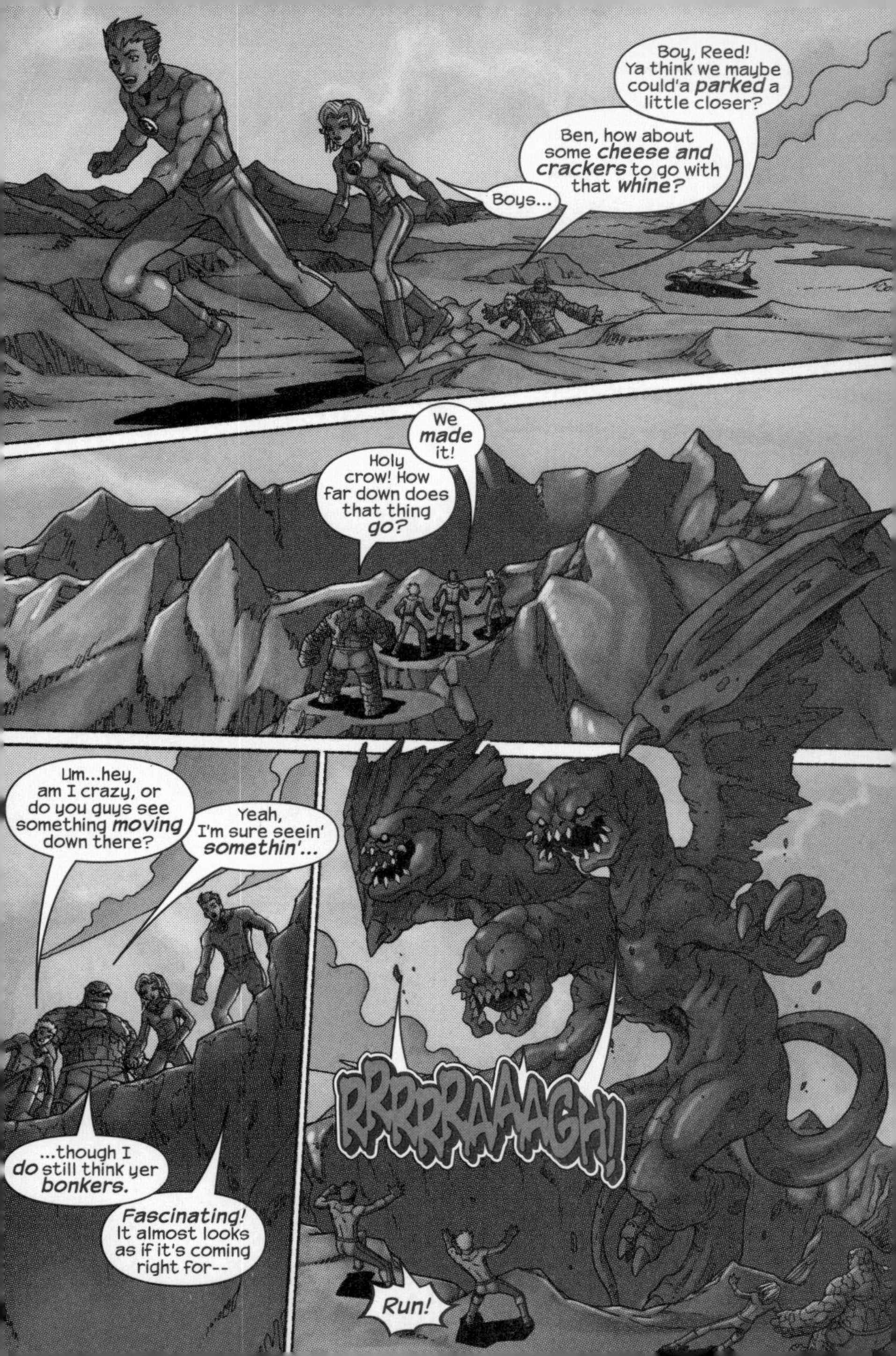
Boy, Reed! Ya think we maybe could'a parked a little closer?
Ben, how about some cheese and crackers to go with that whine?
Boys...
We made it!
Holy crow! How far down does that thing go?
Um...hey, am I crazy, or do you guys see something moving down there?
Yeah, I'm sure seein' somethin'...
...though I do still think yer bonkers.
Fascinating! It almost looks as if it's coming right for--
RRRRRAAAGH!
Run!

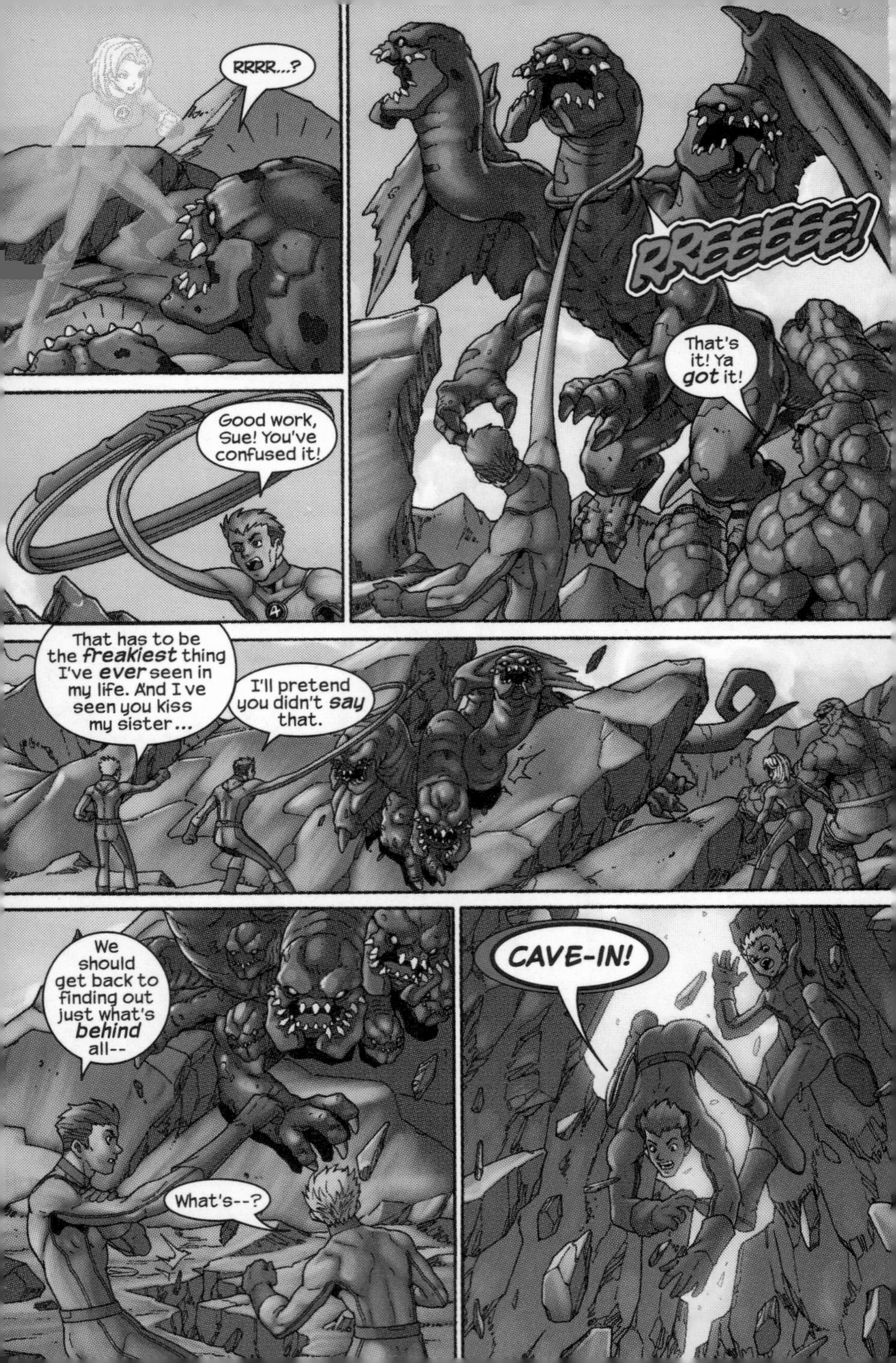

RRRR...?
RREEEEEE!
That's it! Ya got it!
Good work, Sue! You've confused it!
That has to be the freakiest thing I've ever seen in my life. And I ve seen you kiss my sister...
I'll pretend you didn't say that.
We should get back to finding out just what's behind all--
What's--?
CAVE-IN!

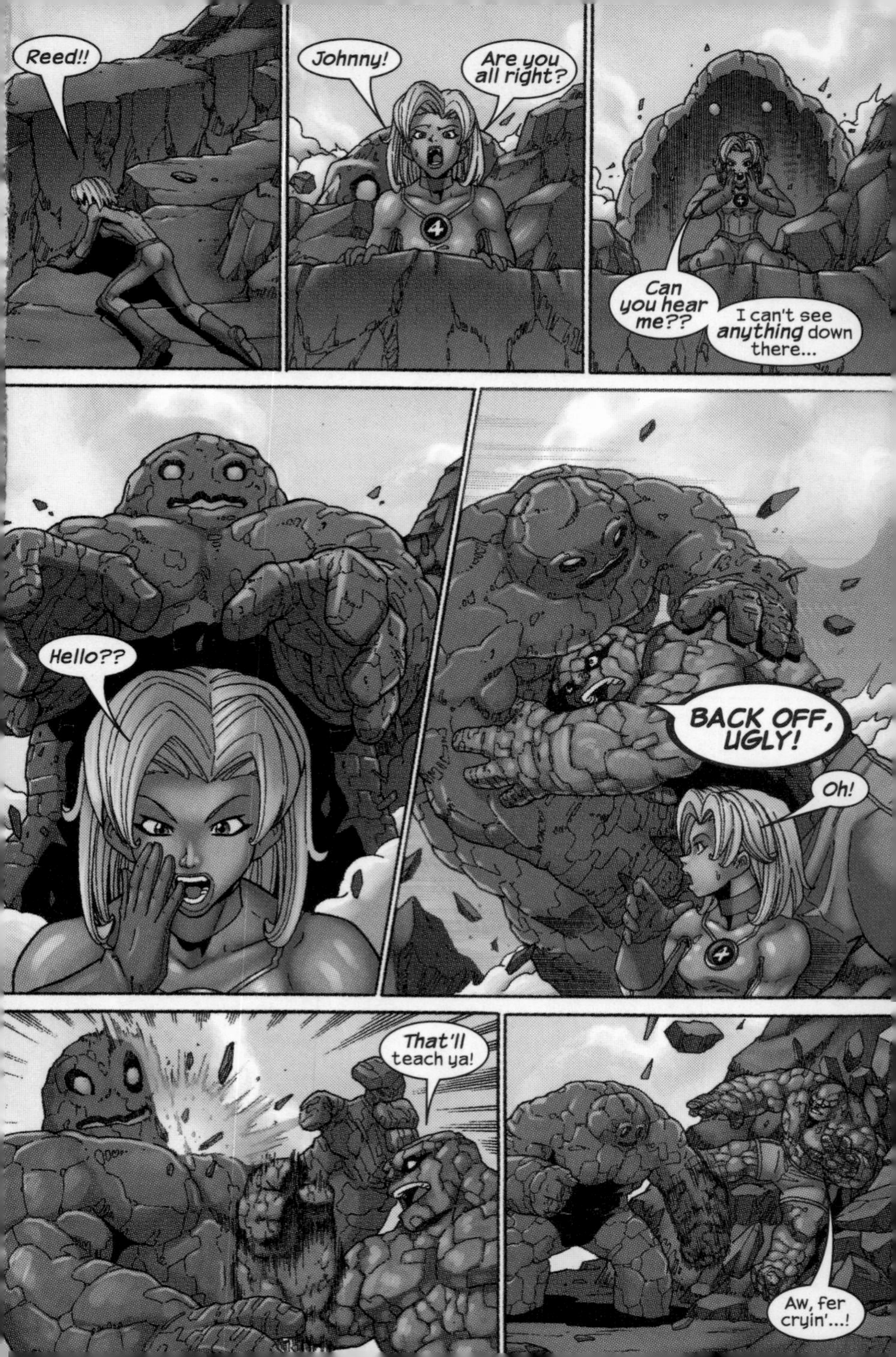
Reed!!
Johnny!
Are you all right?
Can you hear me??
I can't see anything down there...
Hello??
BACK OFF, UGLY!
Oh!
That'll teach ya!
Aw, fer cryin'...!

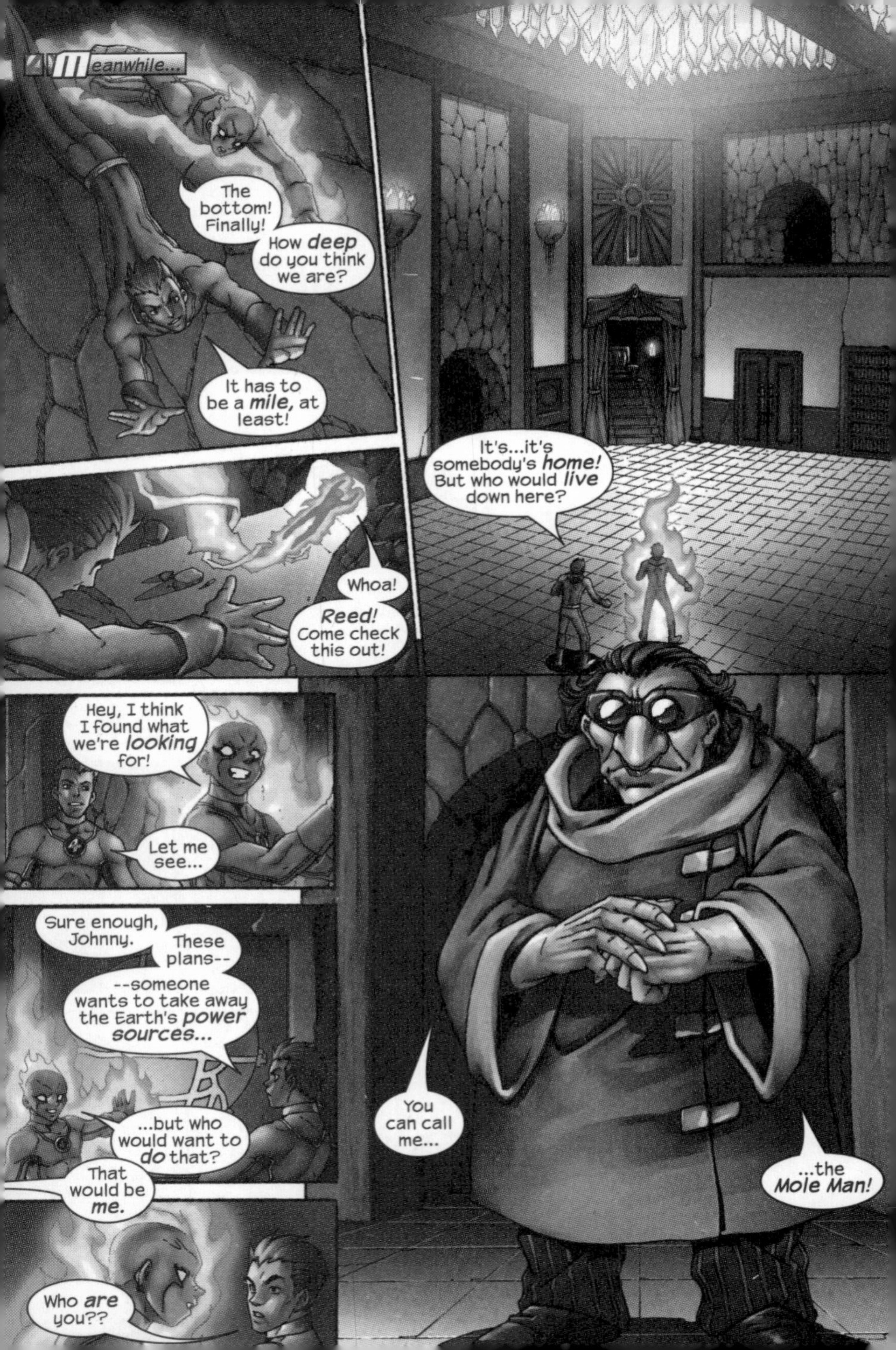
Meanwhile...
The bottom! Finally!
How deep do you think we are?
It has to be a mile, at least!
Whoa!
Reed! Come check this out!
It's...it's somebody's home! But who would live down here?
Hey, I think I found what we're looking for!
Let me see...
Sure enough, Johnny.
These plans--
--someone wants to take away the Earth's power sources...
...but who would want to do that?
That would be me.
Who are you??
You can call me...
...the Mole Man!

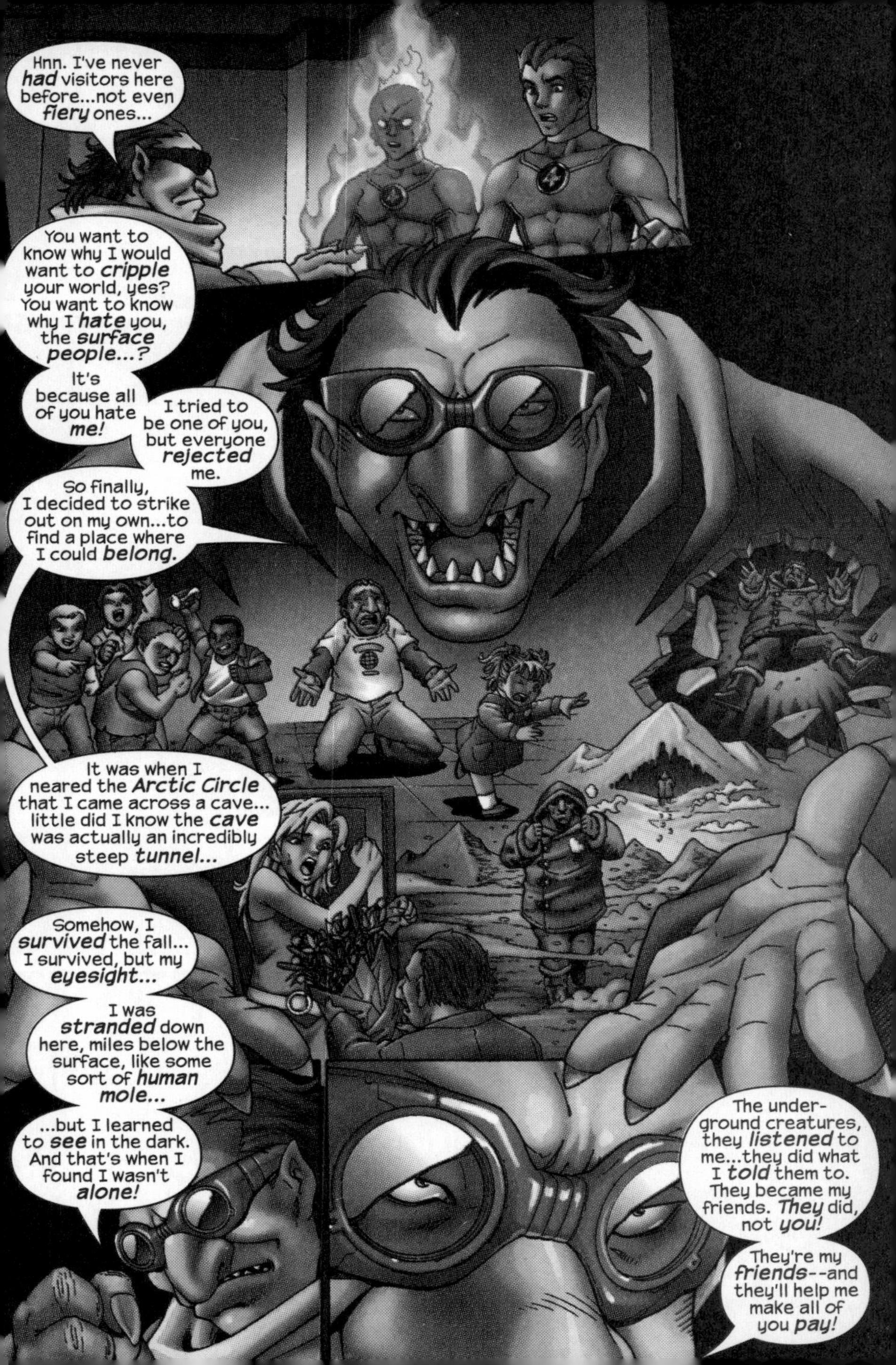
Hnn. I've never had visitors here before...not even fiery ones...
You want to know why I would want to cripple your world, yes? You want to know why I hate you, the surface people...?
It's because all of you hate me!
I tried to be one of you, but everyone rejected me.
So finally, I decided to strike out on my own...to find a place where I could belong.
It was when I neared the Arctic Circle that I came across a cave... little did I know the cave was actually an incredibly steep tunnel...
Somehow, I survived the fall... I survived, but my eyesight...
I was stranded down here, miles below the surface, like some sort of human mole...
...but I learned to see in the dark. And that's when I found I wasn't alone!
The underground creatures, they listened to me...they did what I told them to. They became my friends. They did, not you!
They're my friends--and they'll help me make all of you pay!

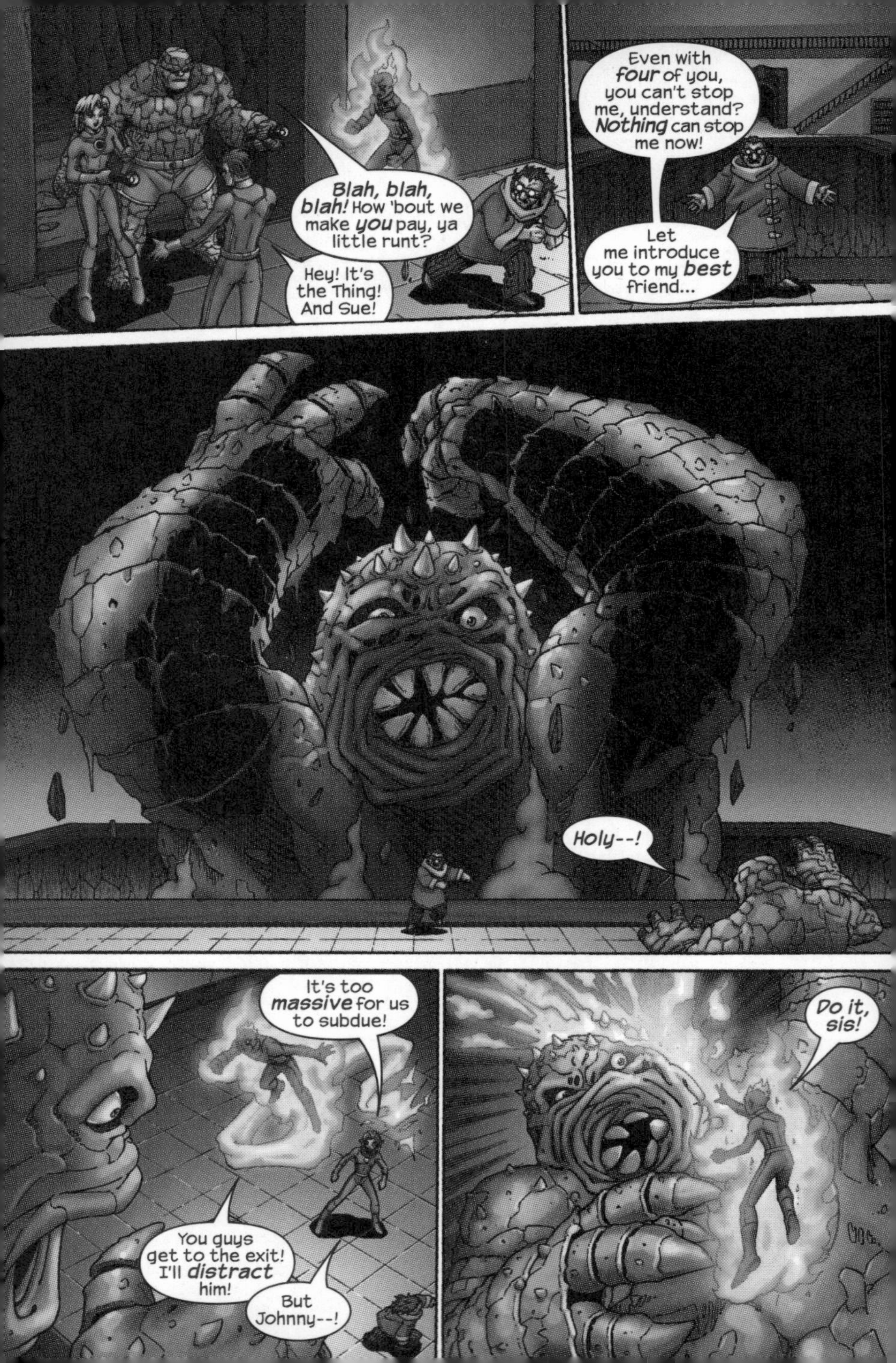
Hey! It's the Thing! And Sue!
Blah, blah, blah! How 'bout we make you pay, ya little runt?
Even with four of you, you can't stop me, understand? Nothing can stop me now!
Let me introduce you to my best friend...
Holy--!
It's too massive for us to subdue!
You guys get to the exit! I'll distract him!
But Johnny--!
Do it, sis!

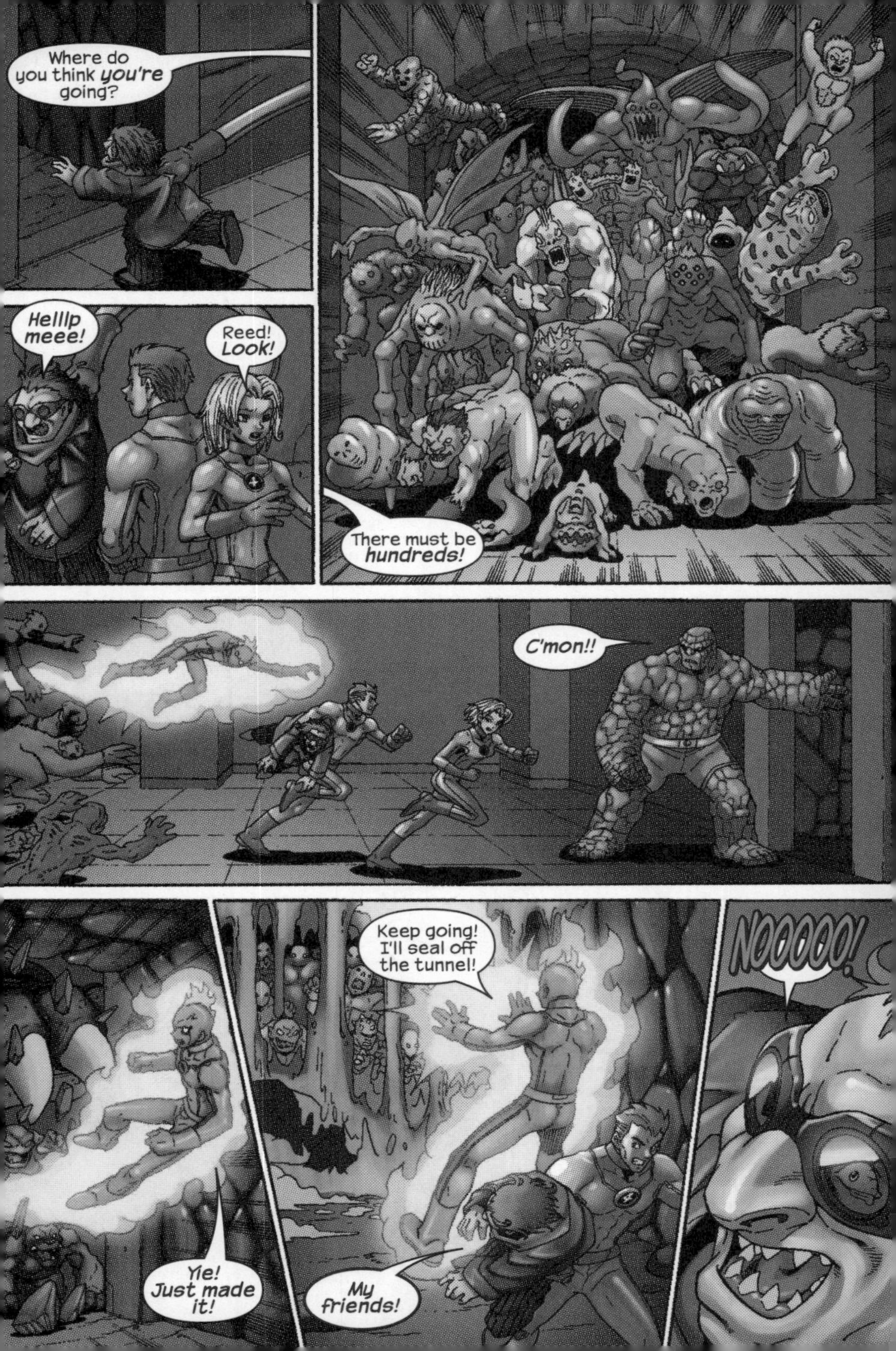
Where do you think you're going?
Helllp meee!
Reed! Look!
There must be hundreds!
C'mon!!
Yie! Just made it!
Keep going! I'll seal off the tunnel!
My friends!
NOOOOO!

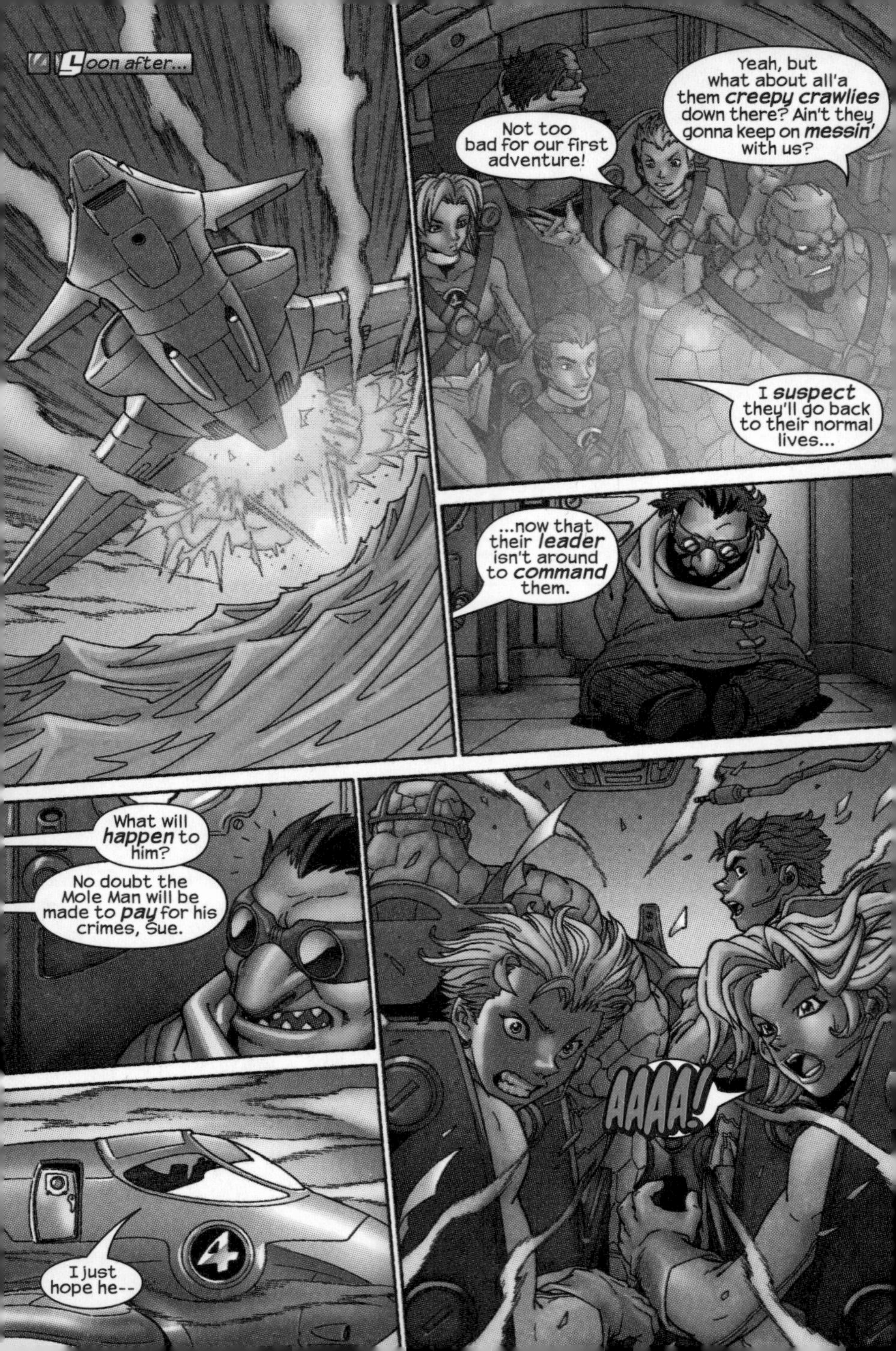
Soon after...
Not too bad for our first adventure!
Yeah, but what about all'a them creepy crawlies down there? Ain't they gonna keep on messin' with us?
I suspect they'll go back to their normal lives...
...now that their leader isn't around to command them.
What will happen to him?
No doubt the Mole Man will be made to pay for his crimes, Sue.
I just hope he--
AAAA!

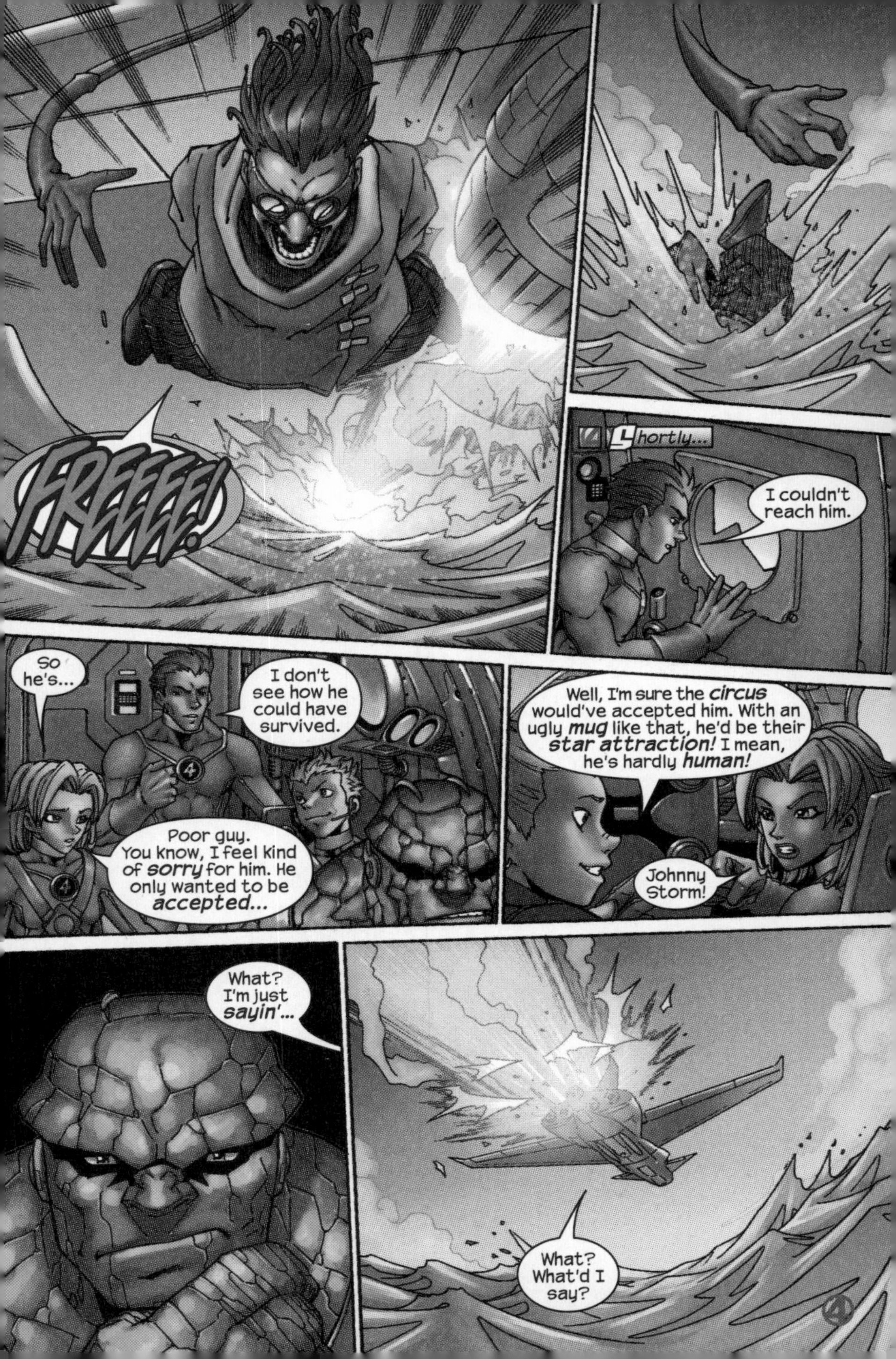
FREEEE!
Shortly...
I couldn't reach him.
So he's...
I don't see how he could have survived.
Poor guy. You know, I feel kind of sorry for him. He only wanted to be accepted...
Well, I'm sure the circus would've accepted him. With an ugly mug like that, he'd be their star attraction! I mean, he's hardly human!
Johnny Storm!
What? I'm just sayin'...
What? What'd I say?

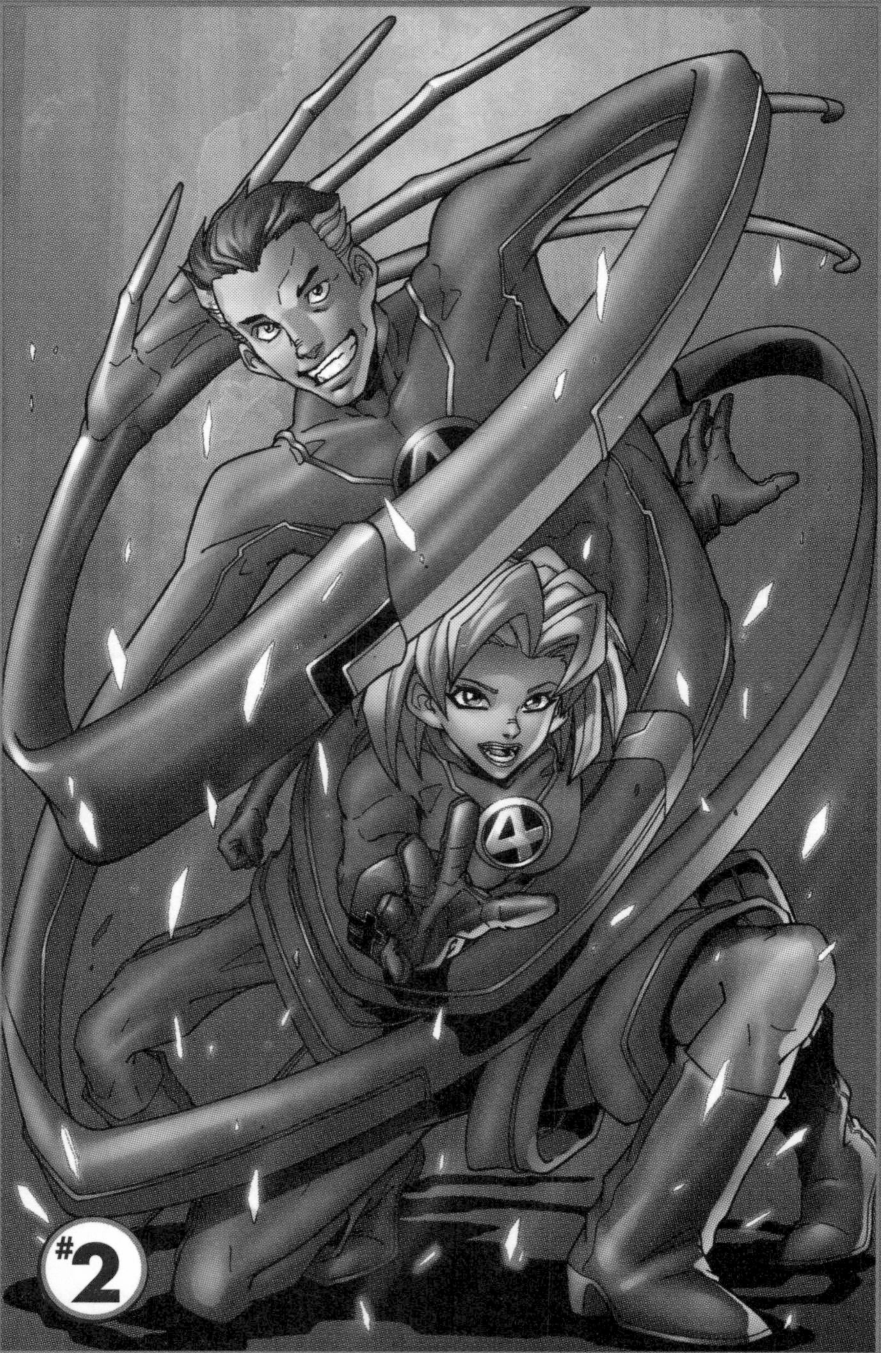
#2

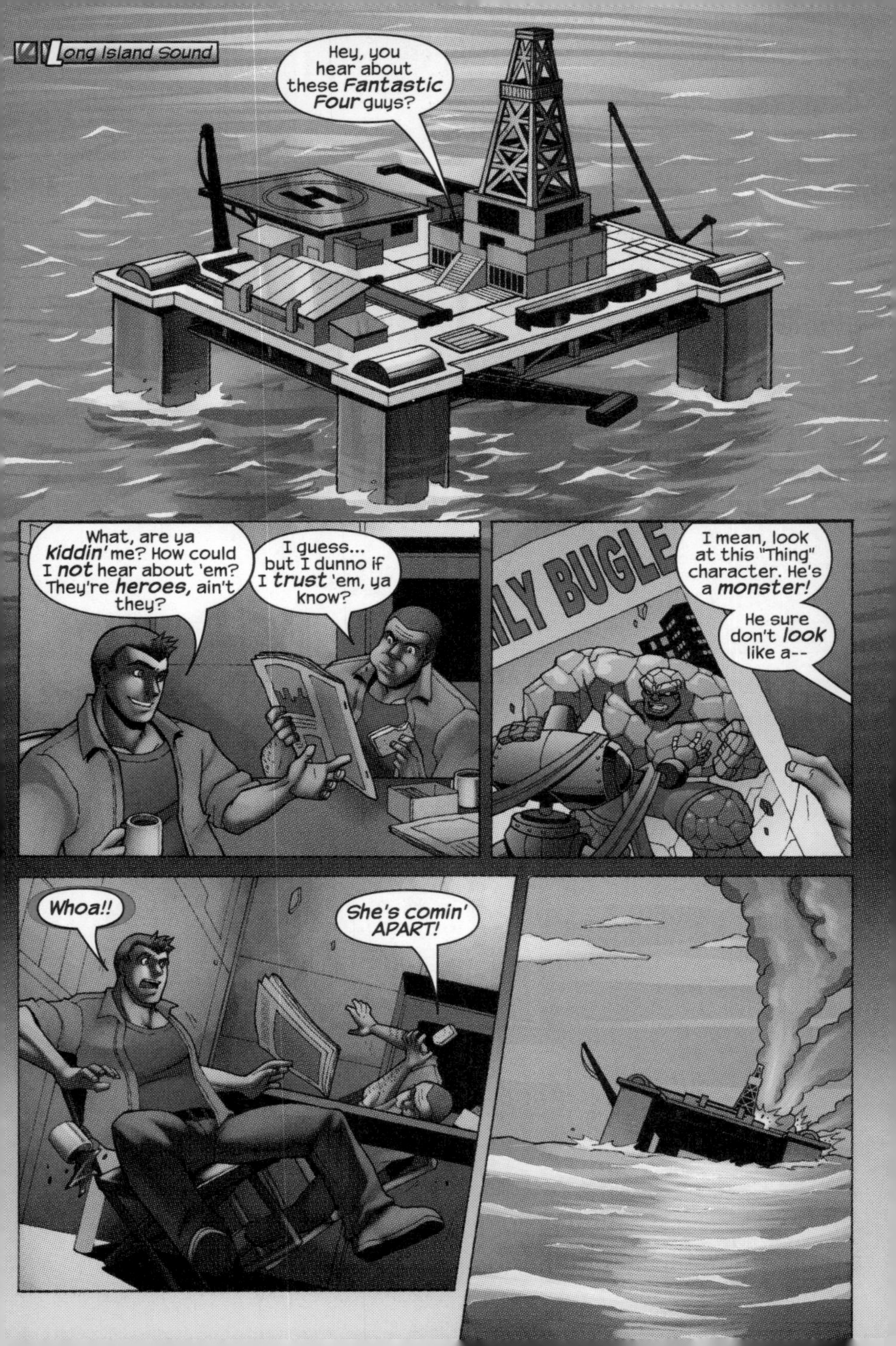
Long Island Sound
Hey, you hear about these Fantastic Four guys?
What, are ya kiddin' me? How could I not hear about 'em? They're heroes, ain't they?
I guess... but I dunno if I trust 'em, ya know?
DAILY BUGLE
I mean, look at this "Thing" character. He's a monster!
He sure don't look like a--
Whoa!!
She's comin' APART!

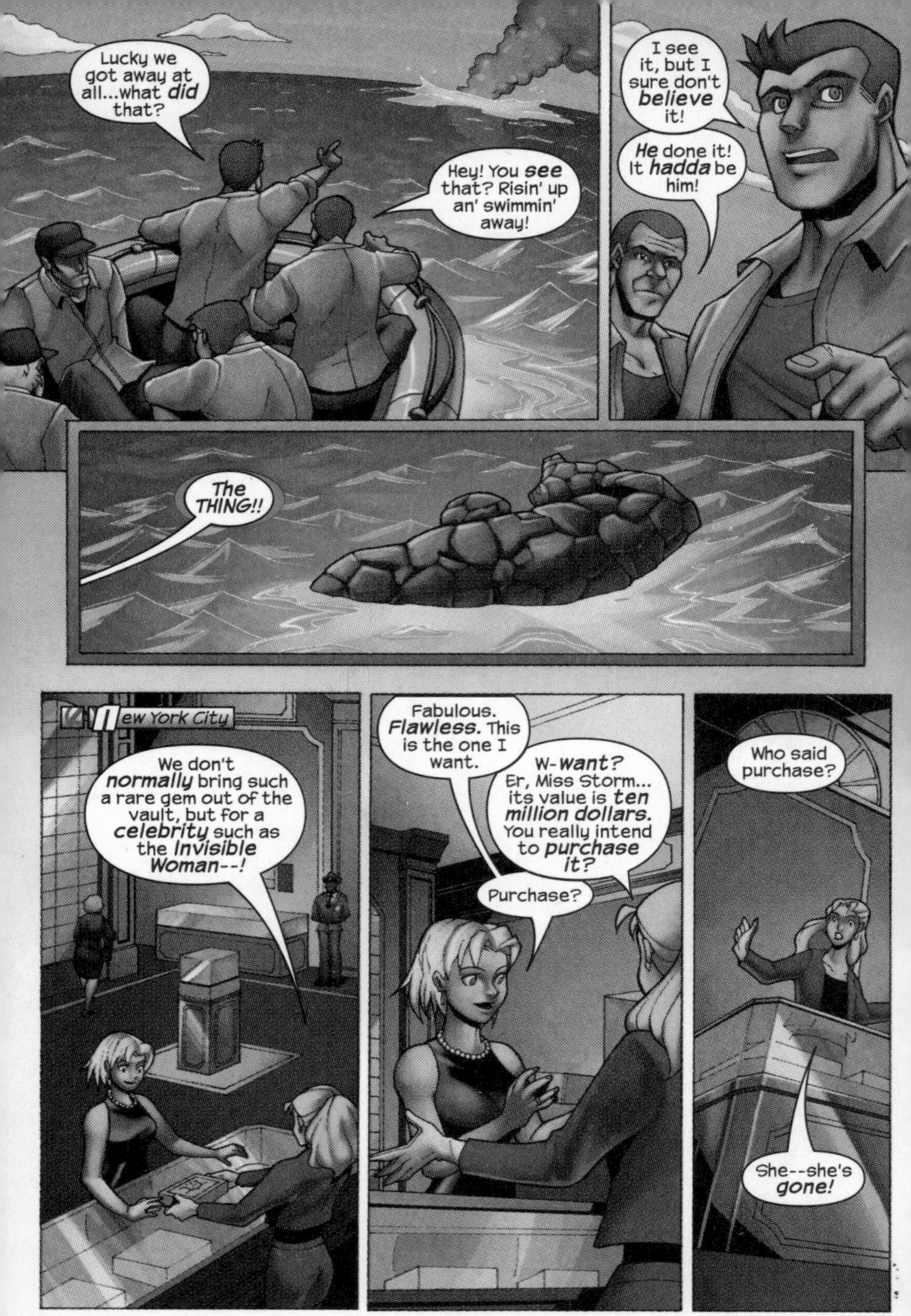
Lucky we got away at all...what did that?
Hey! You see that? Risin' up an' swimmin' away!
I see it, but I sure don't believe it!
He done it! It hadda be him!
The THING!!
New York City
We don't normally bring such a rare gem out of the vault, but for a celebrity such as the Invisible Woman--!
Fabulous. Flawless. This is the one I want.
W-want? Er, Miss Storm... its value is ten million dollars. You really intend to purchase it?
Purchase?
Who said purchase?
She--she's gone!

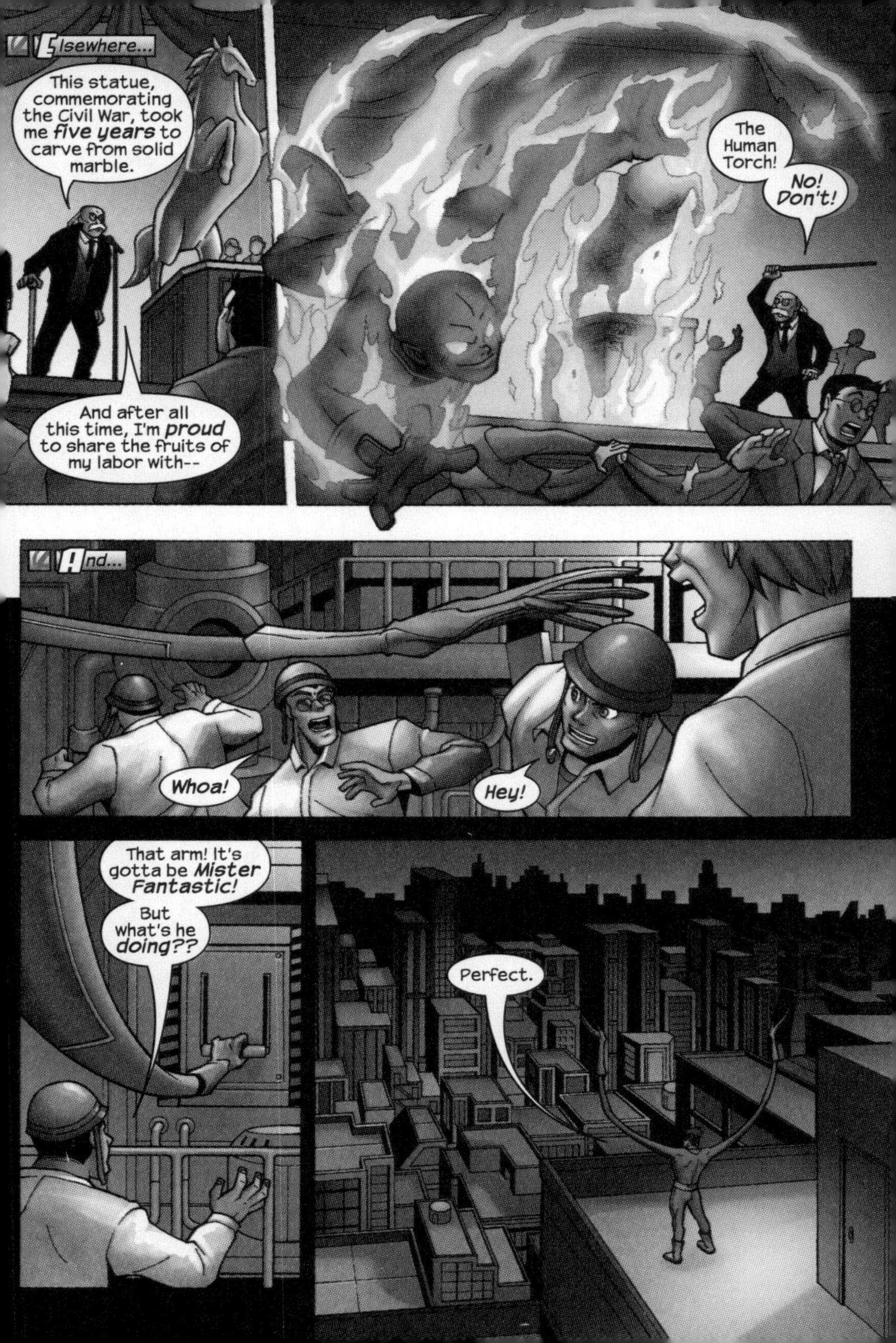
Elsewhere...
This statue, commemorating the Civil War, took me five years to carve from solid marble.
And after all this time, I'm proud to share the fruits of my labor with--
The Human Torch!
No! Don't!
And...
Whoa!
Hey!
That arm! It's gotta be Mister Fantastic!
But what's he doing??
Perfect.

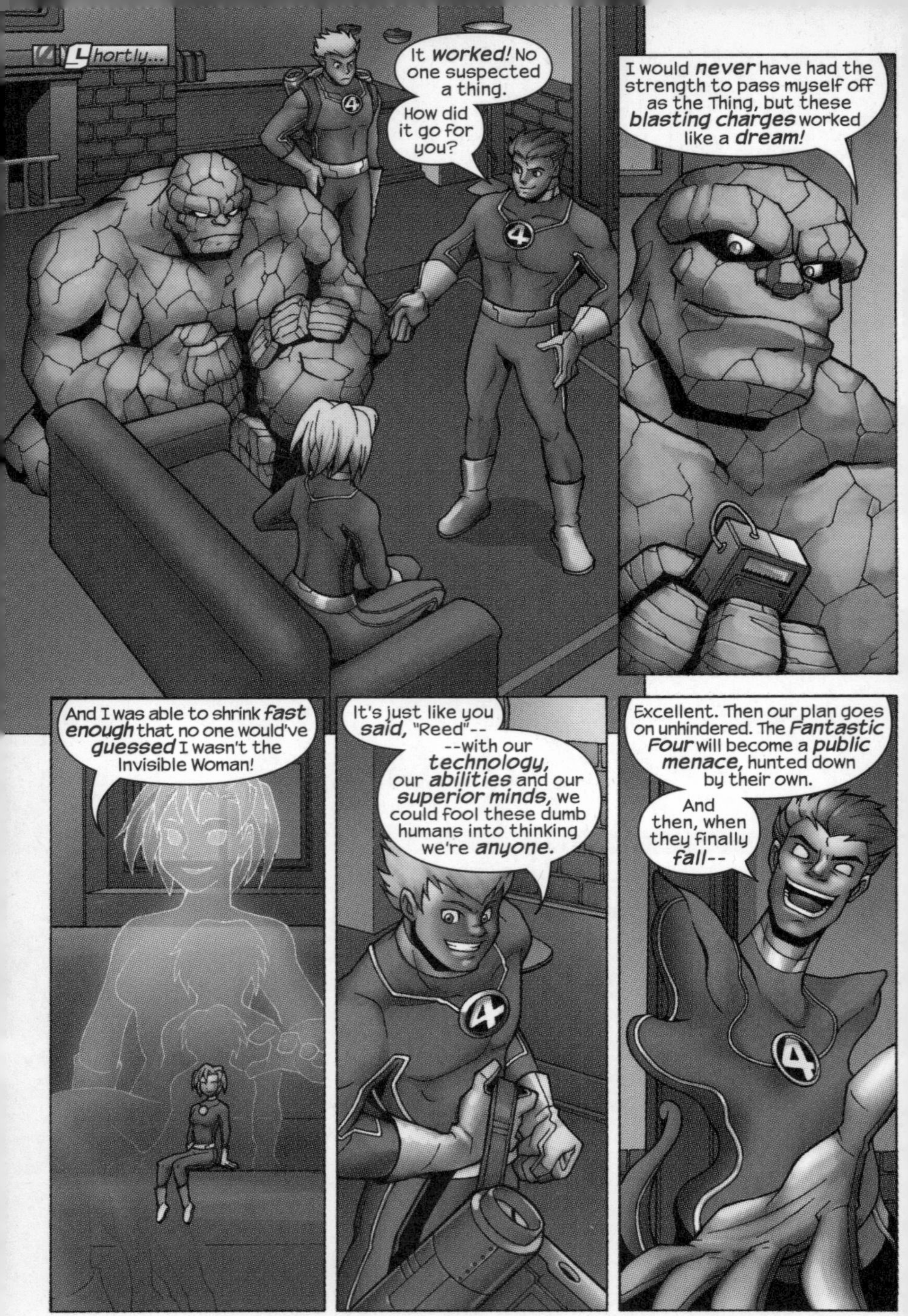
Shortly...
It worked! No one suspected a thing.
How did it go for you?
I would never have had the strength to pass myself off as the Thing, but these blasting charges worked like a dream!
And I was able to shrink fast enough that no one would've guessed I wasn't the Invisible Woman!
It's just like you said, "Reed"--
--with our technology, our abilities and our superior minds, we could fool these dumb humans into thinking we're anyone.
Excellent. Then our plan goes on unhindered. The Fantastic Four will become a public menace, hunted down by their own.
And then, when they finally fall--

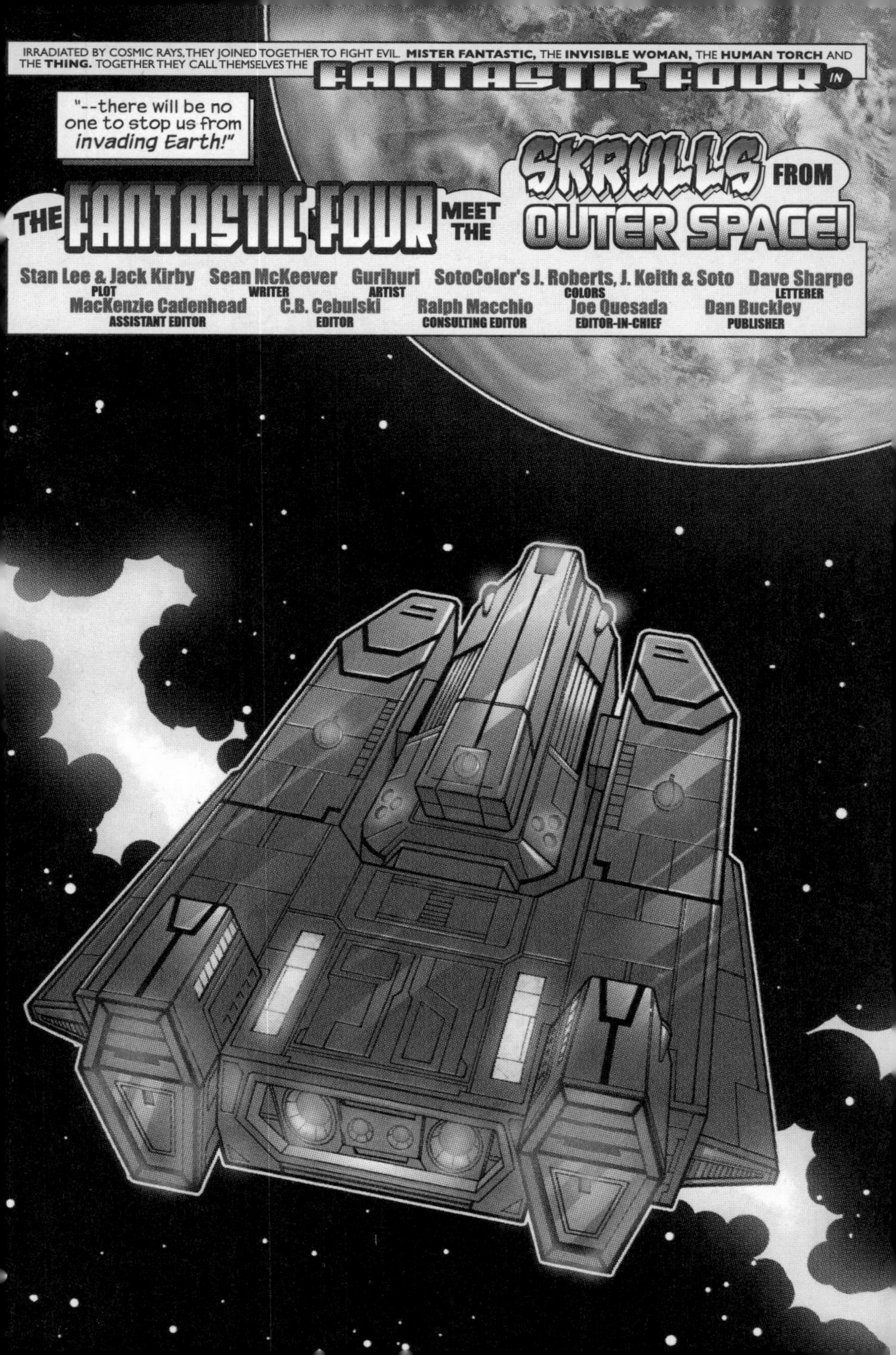

IRRADIATED BY COSMIC RAYS, THEY JOINED TOGETHER TO FIGHT EVIL. MISTER FANTASTIC, THE INVISIBLE WOMAN, THE HUMAN TORCH AND THE THING. TOGETHER THEY CALL THEMSELVES THE FANTASTIC FOUR IN
"--there will be no one to stop us from invading Earth!"
THE FANTASTIC FOUR MEET THE SKRULLS FROM OUTER SPACE!
Stan Lee & Jack Kirby PLOT
Sean McKeever WRITER
Gurihuri ARTIST
SotoColor's J. Roberts, J. Keith & Soto COLORS
Dave Sharpe LETTERER
MacKenzie Cadenhead ASSISTANT EDITOR
C.B. Cebulski EDITOR
Ralph Macchio CONSULTING EDITOR
Joe Quesada EDITOR-IN-CHIEF
Dan Buckley PUBLISHER

Just what in the world is goin' ON here??

FANTASTIC FOUR: PUBLIC ENEMY #1!

You *see* this, Stretch? I never *done* that!

Ben, I know, but--

It's bad enuff that I'm a big, rocky *freak*--

FANTASTIC FOUR: PUBLIC ENEMY #1!

--now I got some jerk-head *tarnishin'* my good name!

*Our* good names! It's enuff ta make me--

Ben! Calm down, pal!

I'm frustrated too, but there's no cause for gratuitous property damage!

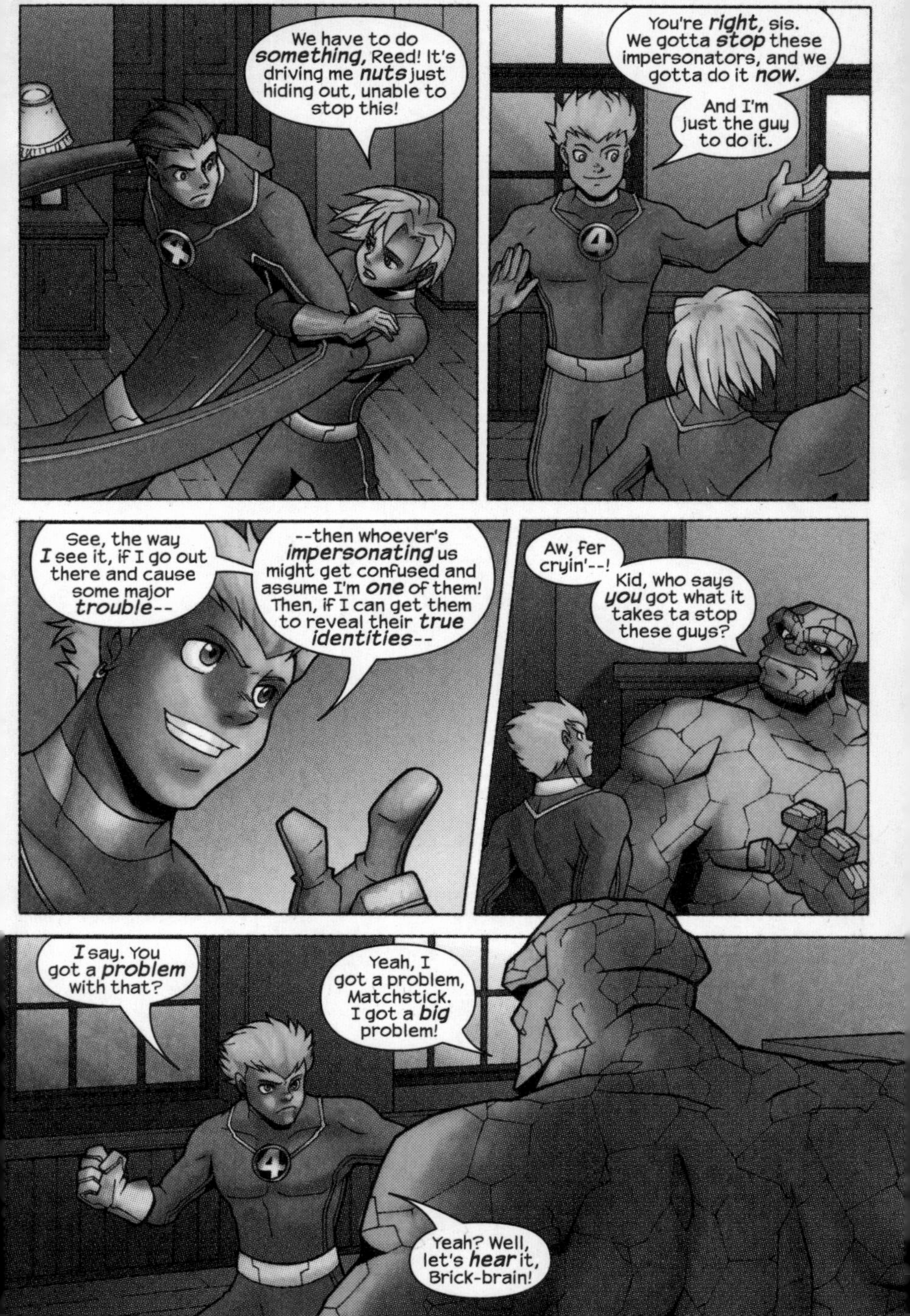
We have to do something, Reed! It's driving me nuts just hiding out, unable to stop this!
You're right, sis. We gotta stop these impersonators, and we gotta do it now.
And I'm just the guy to do it.
See, the way I see it, if I go out there and cause some major trouble--
--then whoever's impersonating us might get confused and assume I'm one of them! Then, if I can get them to reveal their true identities--
Aw, fer cryin'--!
Kid, who says you got what it takes ta stop these guys?
I say. You got a problem with that?
Yeah, I got a problem, Matchstick. I got a big problem!
Yeah? Well, let's hear it, Brick-brain!

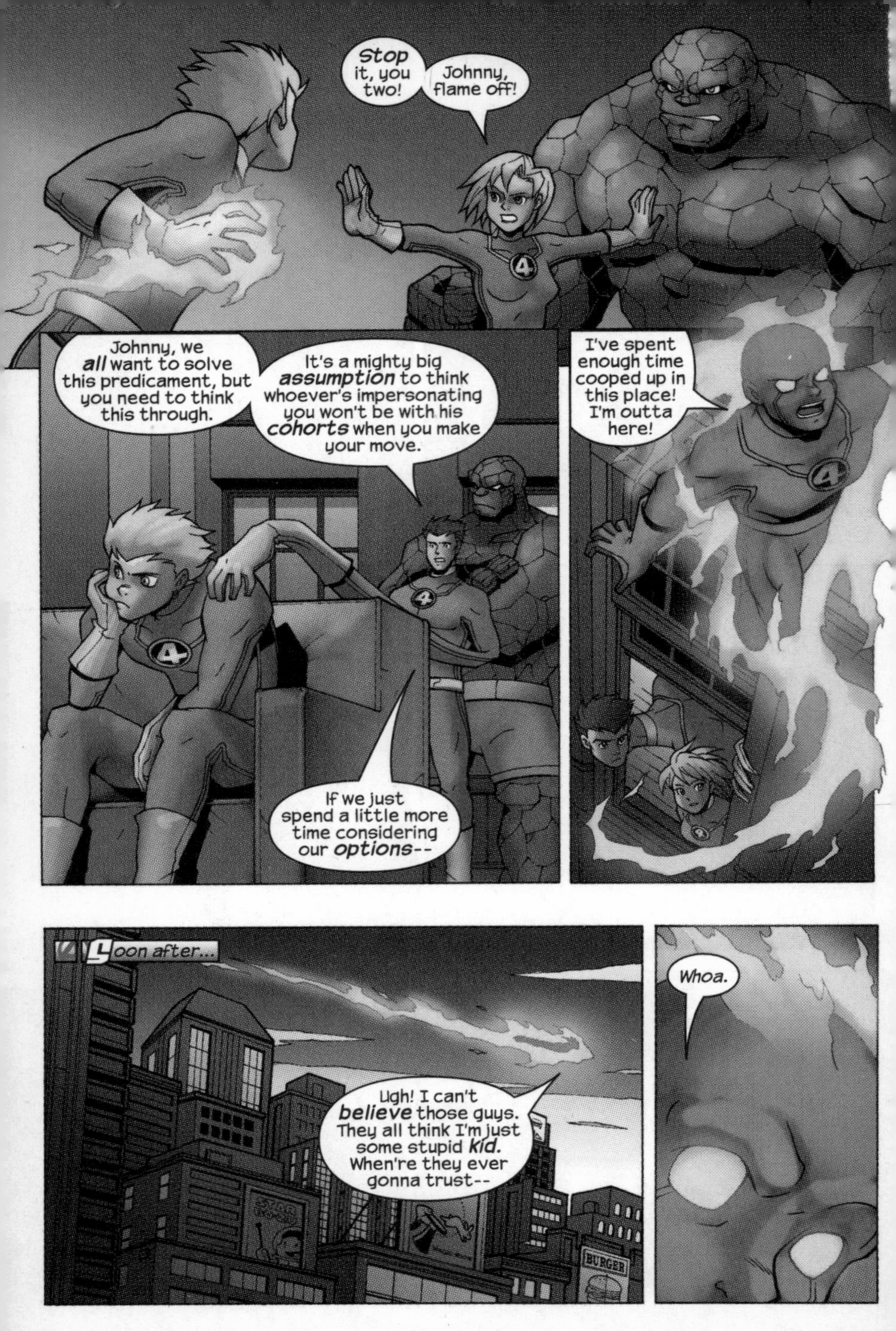
Stop it, you two!
Johnny, flame off!
Johnny, we all want to solve this predicament, but you need to think this through.
It's a mighty big assumption to think whoever's impersonating you won't be with his cohorts when you make your move.
If we just spend a little more time considering our options--
I've spent enough time cooped up in this place! I'm outta here!
Soon after...
Ugh! I can't believe those guys. They all think I'm just some stupid kid. When're they ever gonna trust--
BURGER
Whoa.

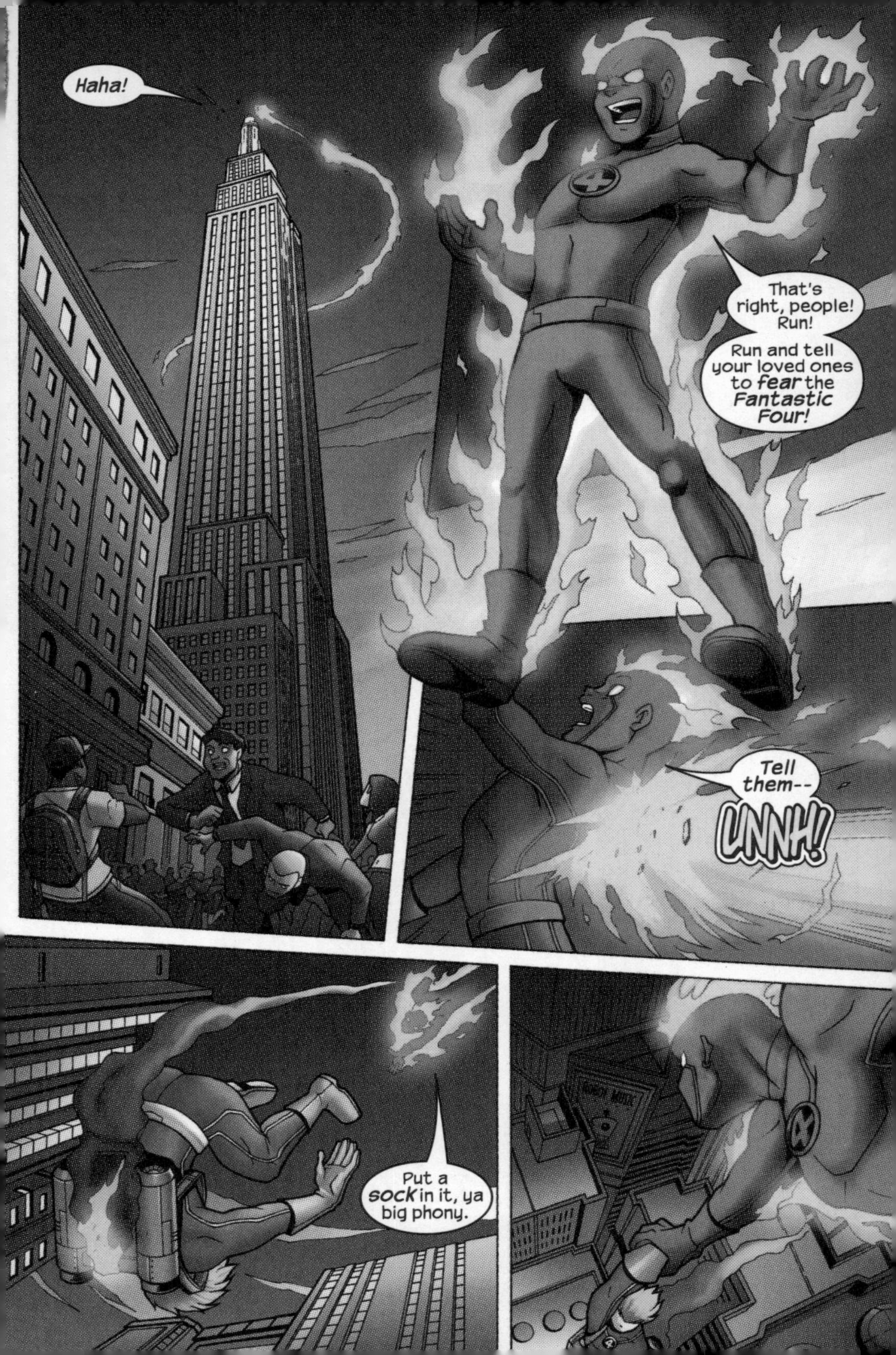

Haha!
That's right, people! Run!
Run and tell your loved ones to fear the Fantastic Four!
Tell them--
UNNH!
Put a sock in it, ya big phony.

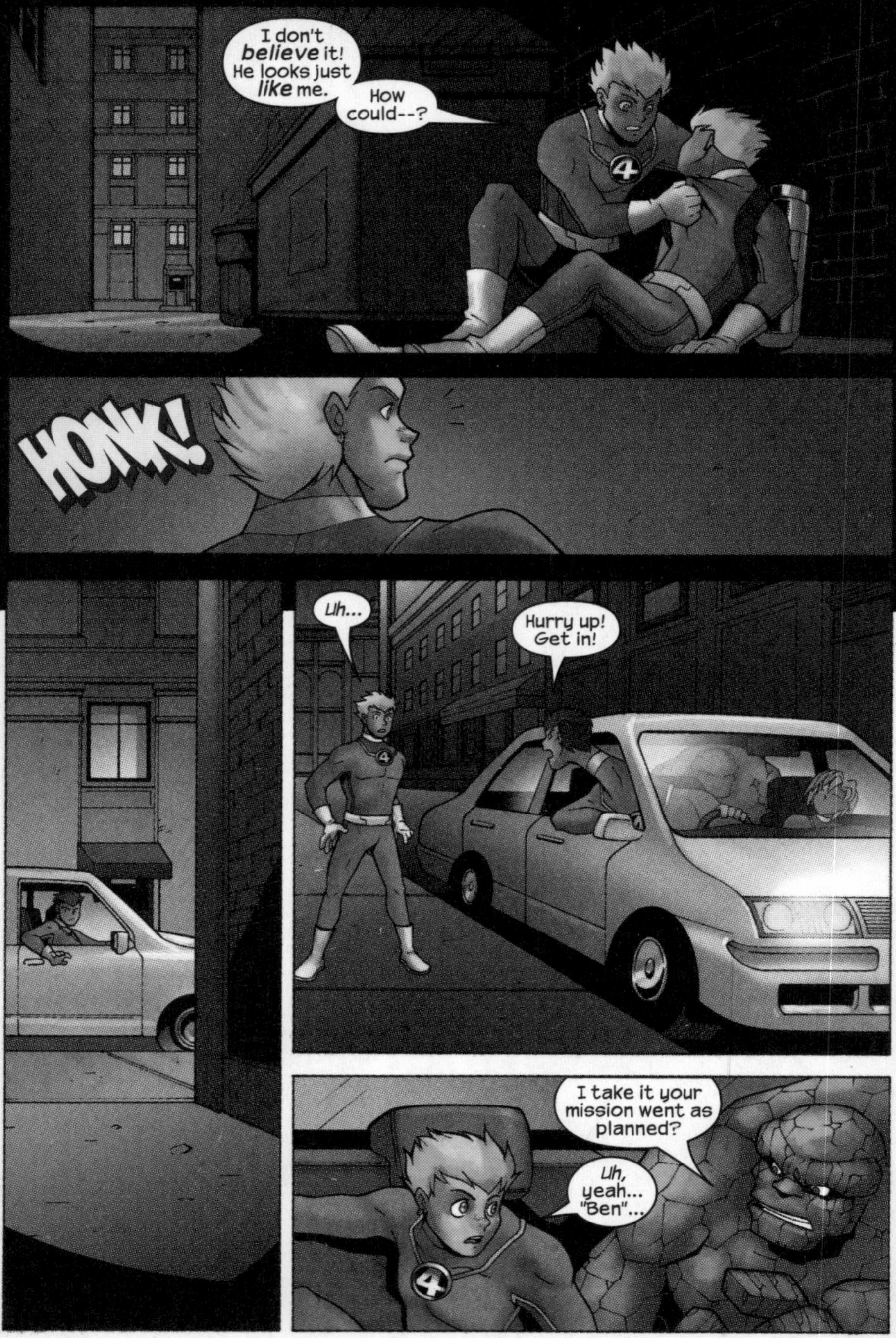

I don't *believe* it! He looks just *like* me.
How could--?
HONK!
Uh...
Hurry up! Get in!
I take it your mission went as planned?
Uh, yeah... "Ben"...

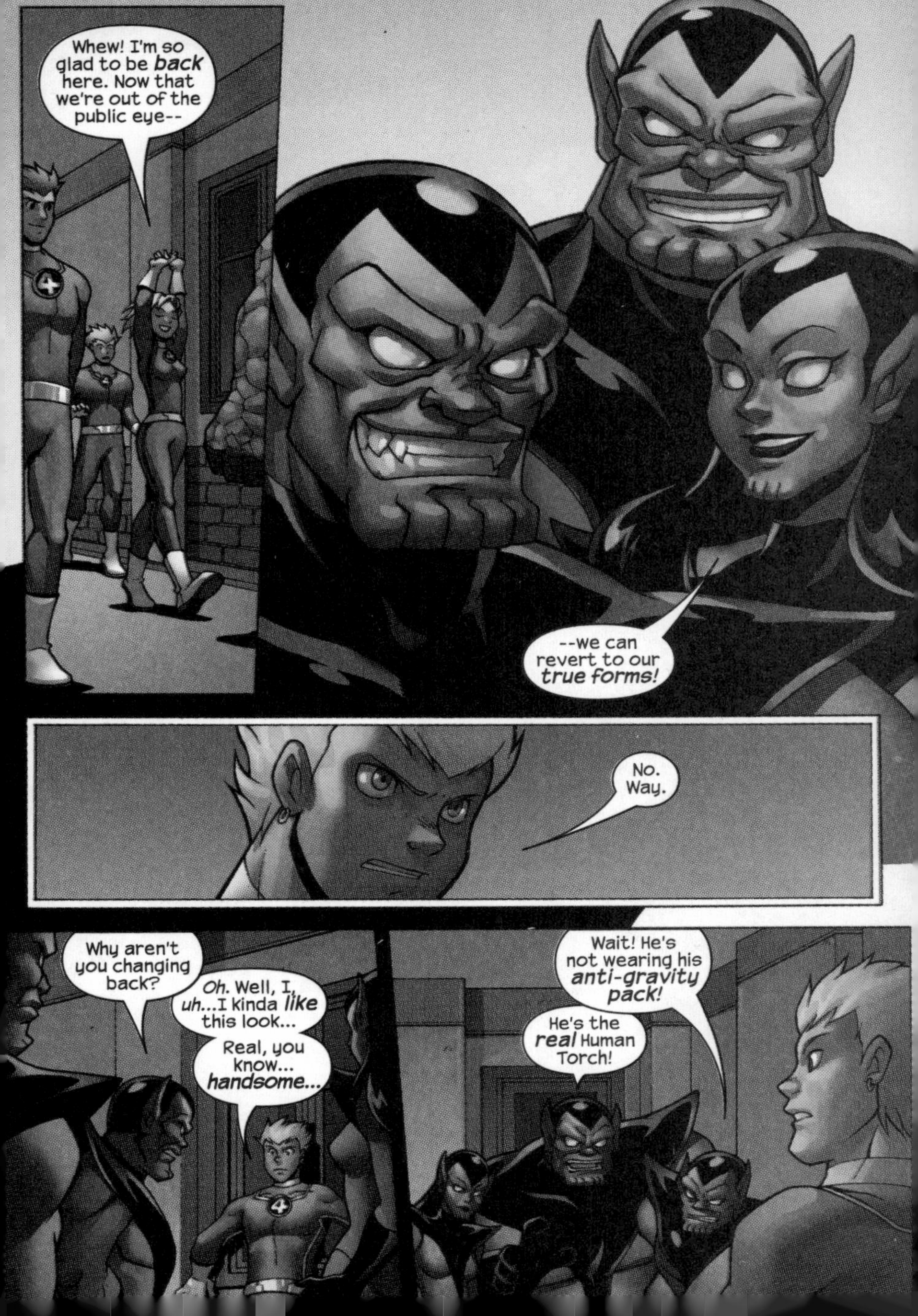
Whew! I'm so glad to be *back* here. Now that we're out of the public eye--
--we can revert to our *true forms!*
No. Way.
Why aren't you changing back?
*Oh.* Well, I, *uh*...I kinda *like* this look...
Real, you know... ***handsome...***
Wait! He's not wearing his ***anti-gravity pack!***
He's the ***real*** Human Torch!

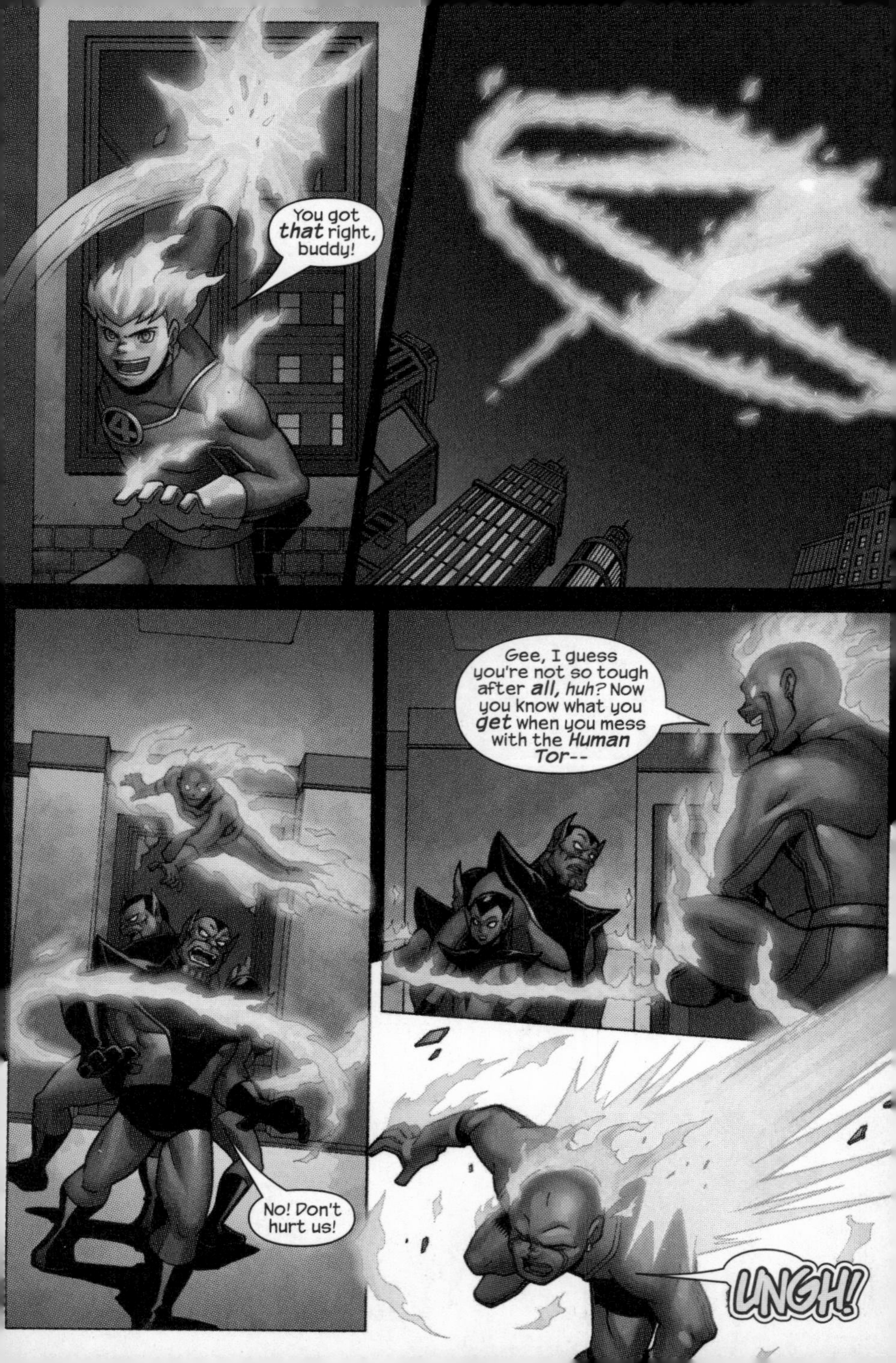
You got *that* right, buddy!
Gee, I guess you're not so tough after *all, huh?* Now you know what you *get* when you mess with the *Human Tor--*
No! Don't hurt us!
UNGH!

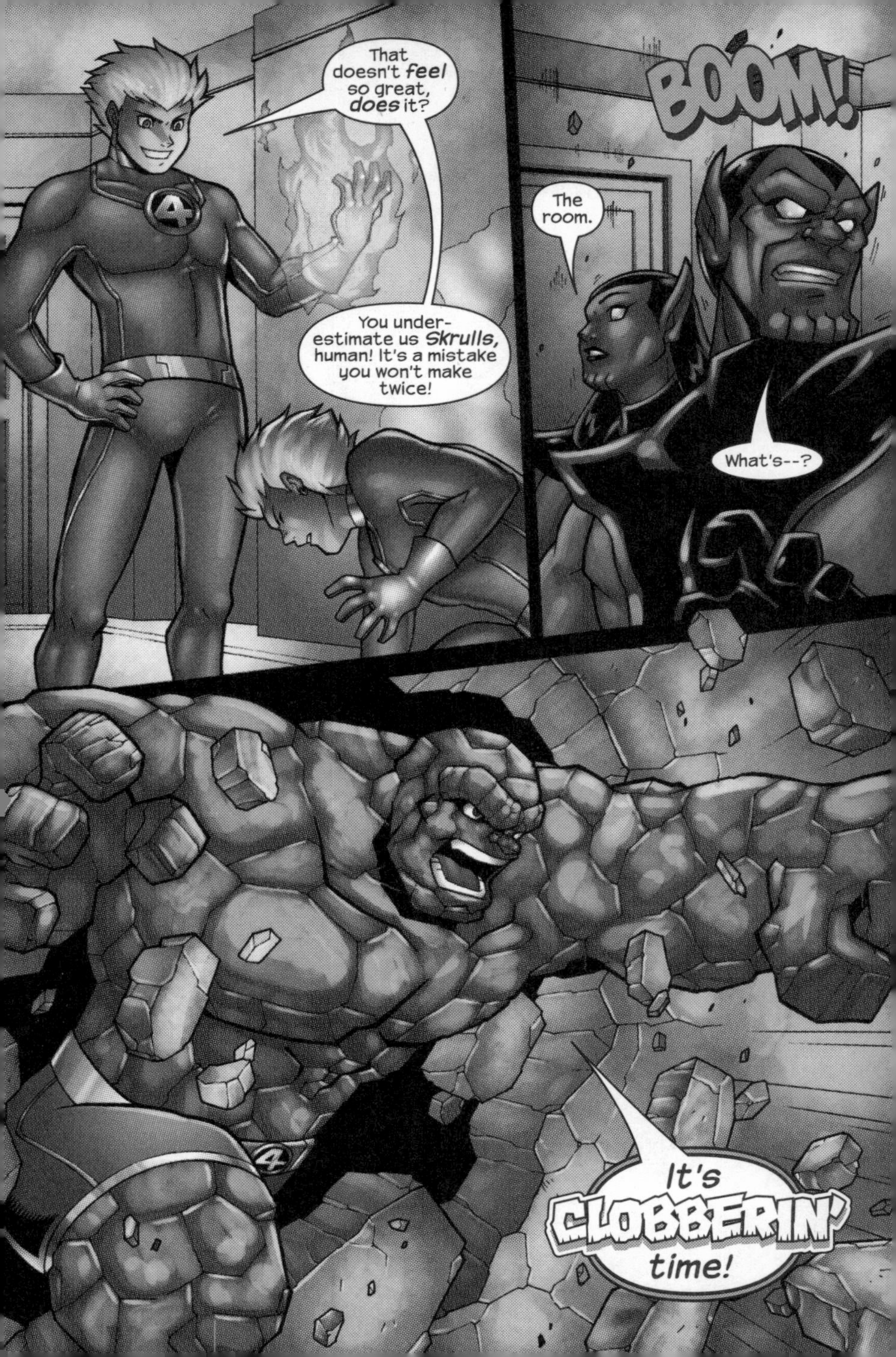
That doesn't *feel* so great, *does* it?
You under-estimate us *Skrulls,* human! It's a mistake you won't make twice!
BOOM!
The room.
What's--?
It's CLOBBERIN' time!

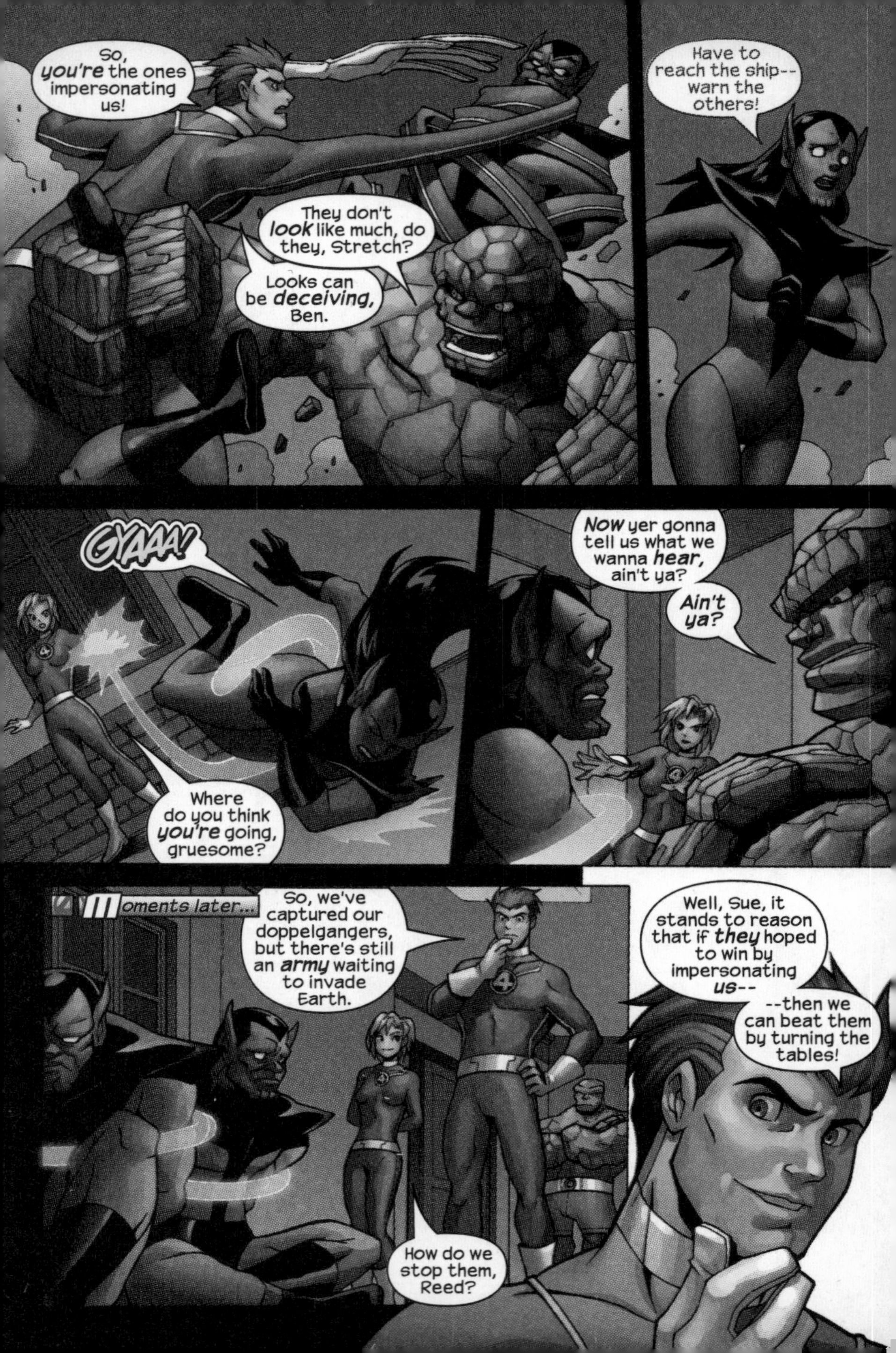
So, you're the ones impersonating us!
They don't look like much, do they, Stretch?
Looks can be deceiving, Ben.
Have to reach the ship--warn the others!
GYAAA!
Where do you think you're going, gruesome?
NOW yer gonna tell us what we wanna hear, ain't ya?
Ain't ya?
Moments later...
So, we've captured our doppelgangers, but there's still an army waiting to invade Earth.
How do we stop them, Reed?
Well, Sue, it stands to reason that if they hoped to win by impersonating us--
--then we can beat them by turning the tables!

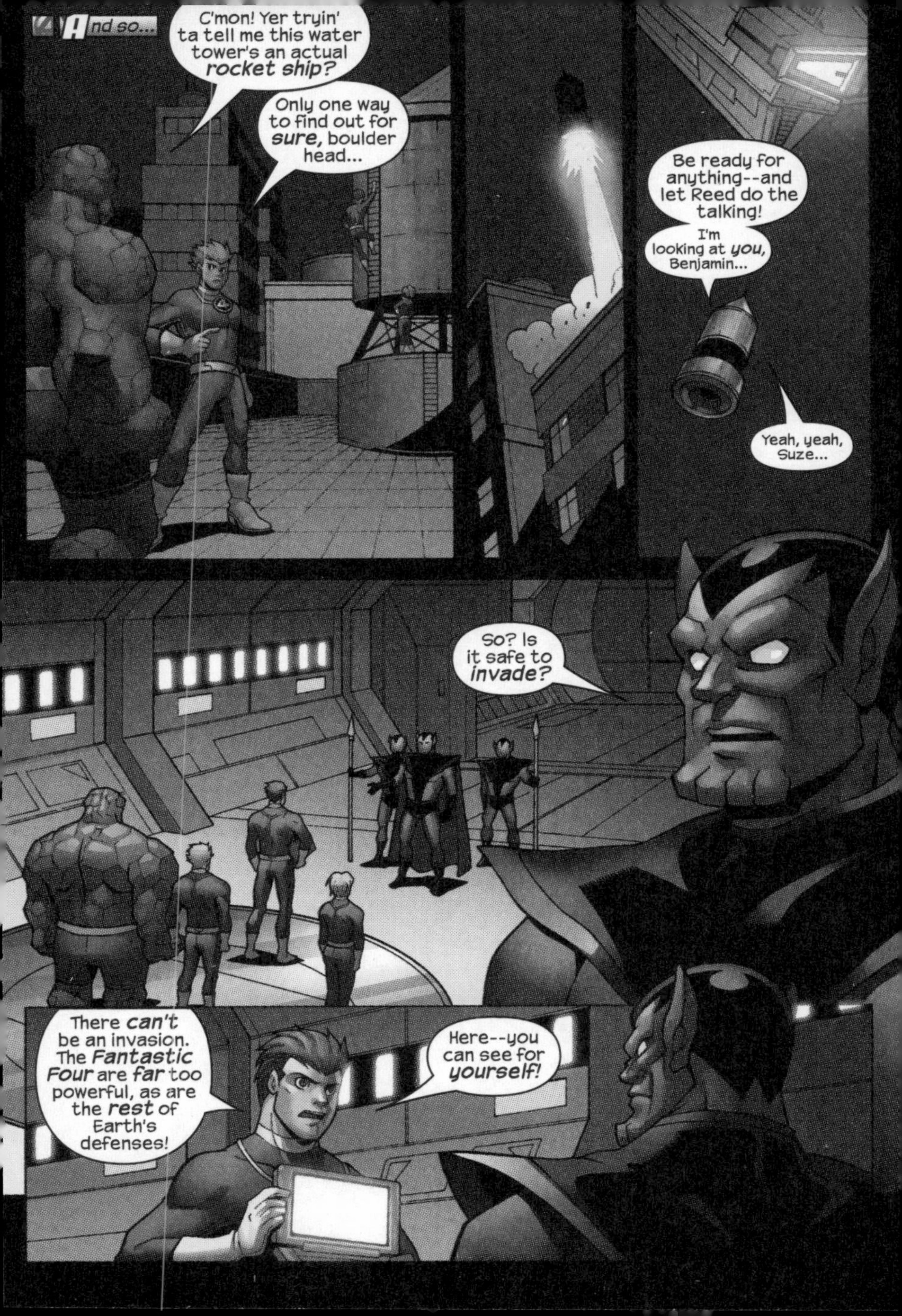
And so...
C'mon! Yer tryin' ta tell me this water tower's an actual rocket ship?
Only one way to find out for sure, boulder head...
Be ready for anything--and let Reed do the talking!
I'm looking at you, Benjamin...
Yeah, yeah, Suze...
So? Is it safe to invade?
There can't be an invasion. The Fantastic Four are far too powerful, as are the rest of Earth's defenses!
Here--you can see for yourself!

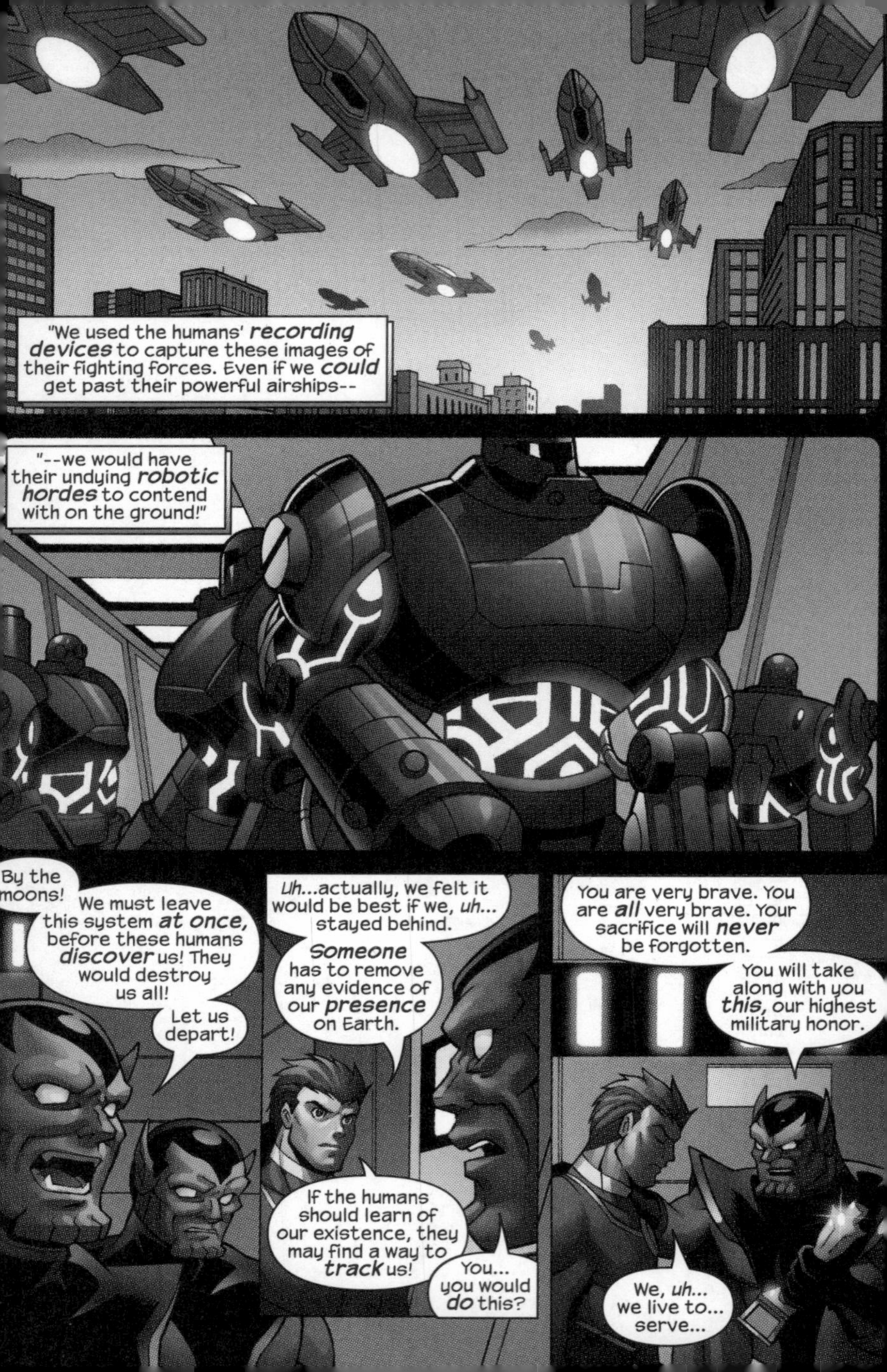
"We used the humans' recording devices to capture these images of their fighting forces. Even if we could get past their powerful airships--
"--we would have their undying robotic hordes to contend with on the ground!"
By the moons!
We must leave this system at once, before these humans discover us! They would destroy us all!
Let us depart!
Uh...actually, we felt it would be best if we, uh... stayed behind.
Someone has to remove any evidence of our presence on Earth.
If the humans should learn of our existence, they may find a way to track us!
You... you would do this?
You are very brave. You are all very brave. Your sacrifice will never be forgotten.
You will take along with you this, our highest military honor.
We, uh... we live to... serve...

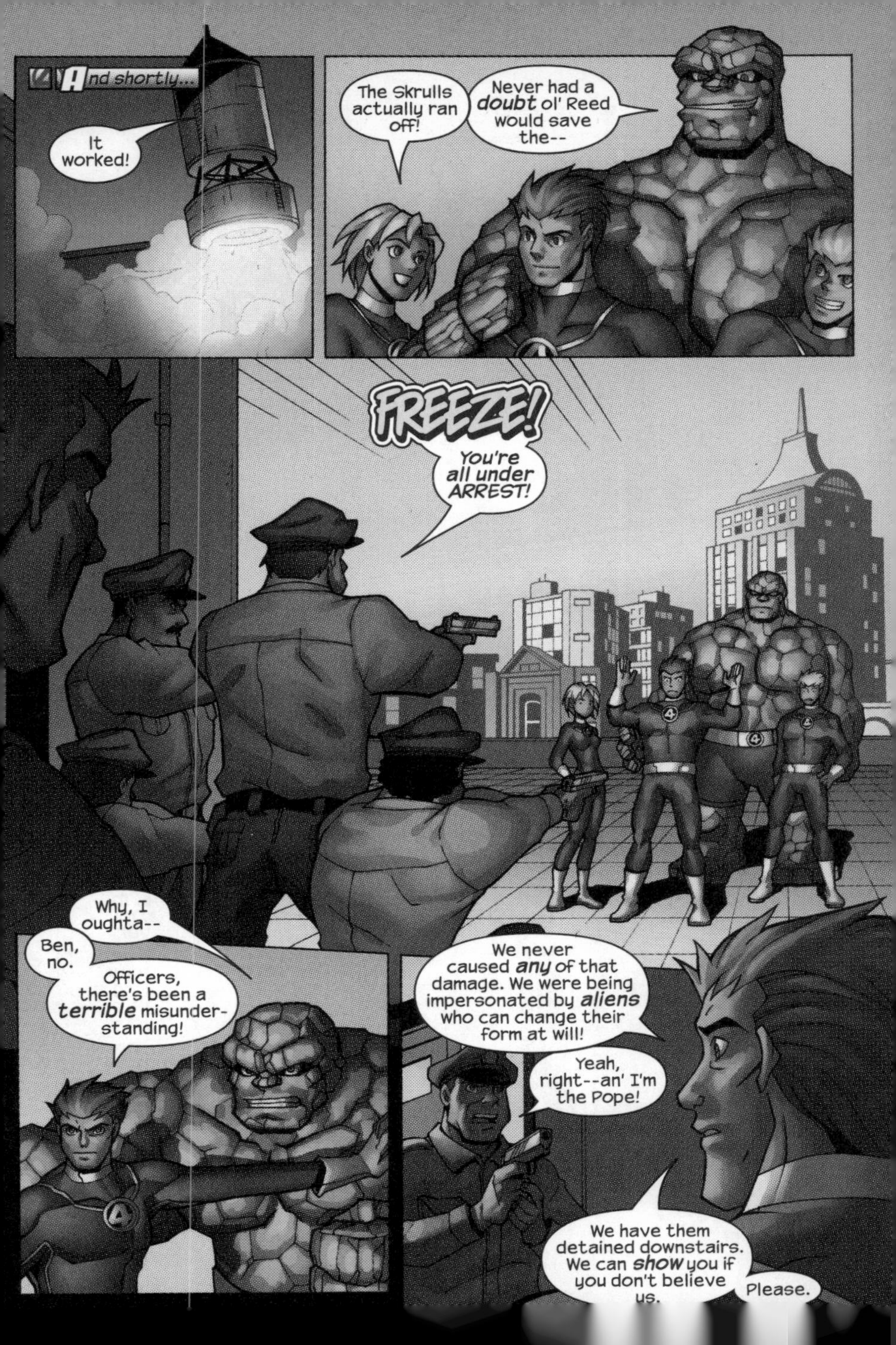
And shortly...
It worked!
The Skrulls actually ran off!
Never had a doubt ol' Reed would save the--
FREEZE!
You're all under ARREST!
Why, I oughta--
Ben, no.
Officers, there's been a terrible misunder-standing!
We never caused any of that damage. We were being impersonated by aliens who can change their form at will!
Yeah, right--an' I'm the Pope!
We have them detained downstairs. We can show you if you don't believe us.
Please.

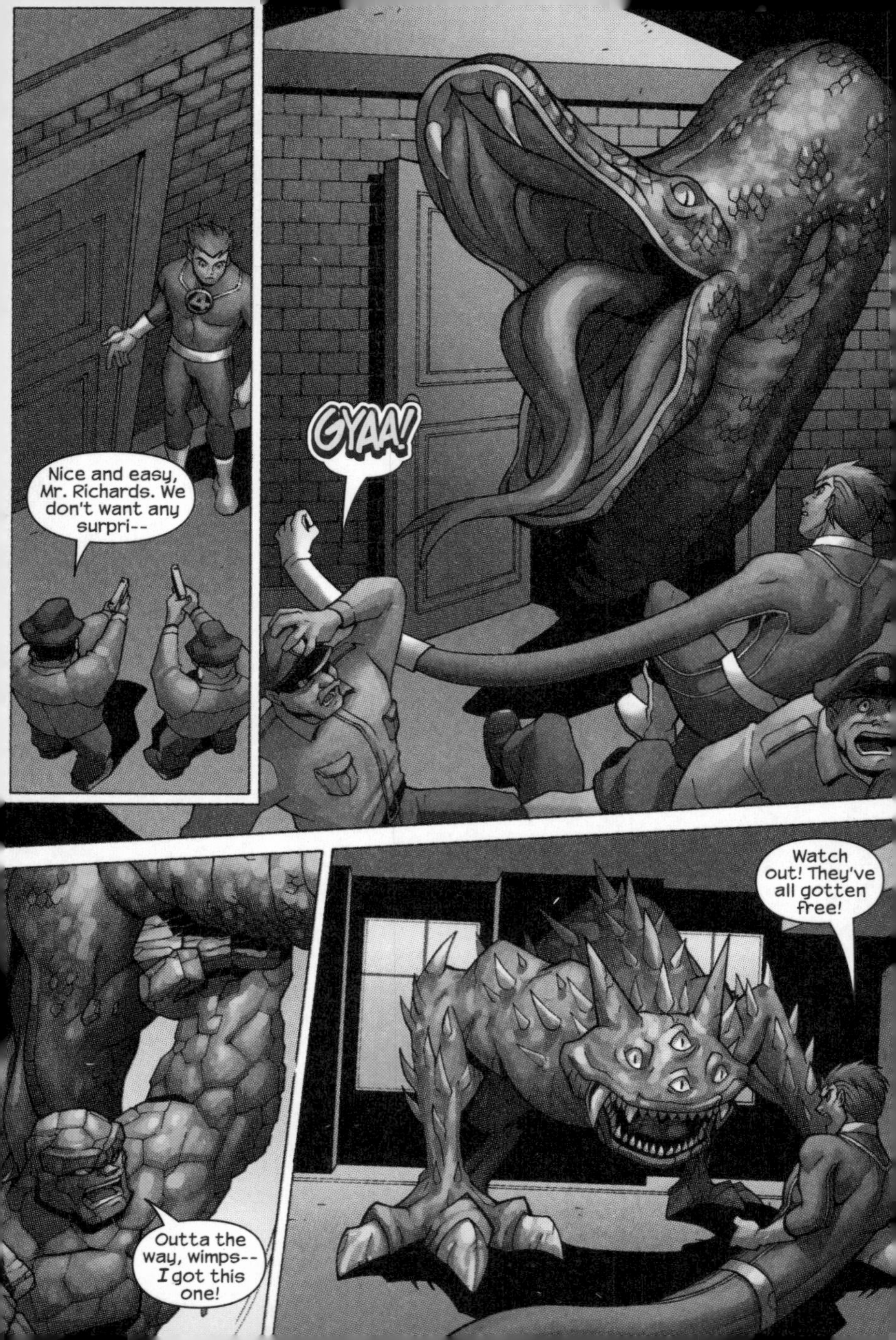
Nice and easy, Mr. Richards. We don't want any surpri--
GYAA!
Outta the way, wimps-- I got this one!
Watch out! They've all gotten free!

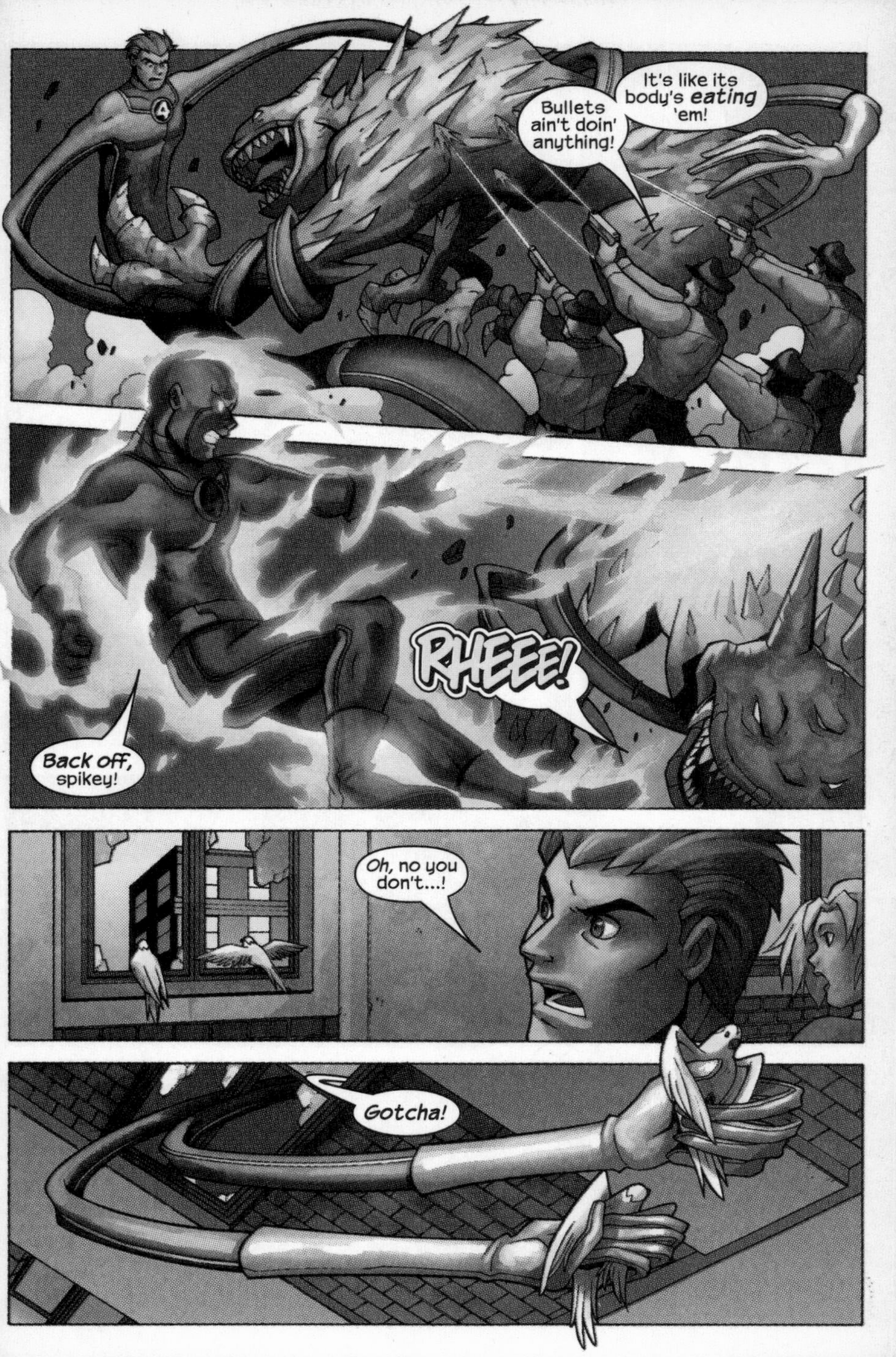
Bullets ain't doin' anything!
It's like its body's *eating* 'em!
Back off, spikey!
RHEEEE!
Oh, no you don't...!
Gotcha!

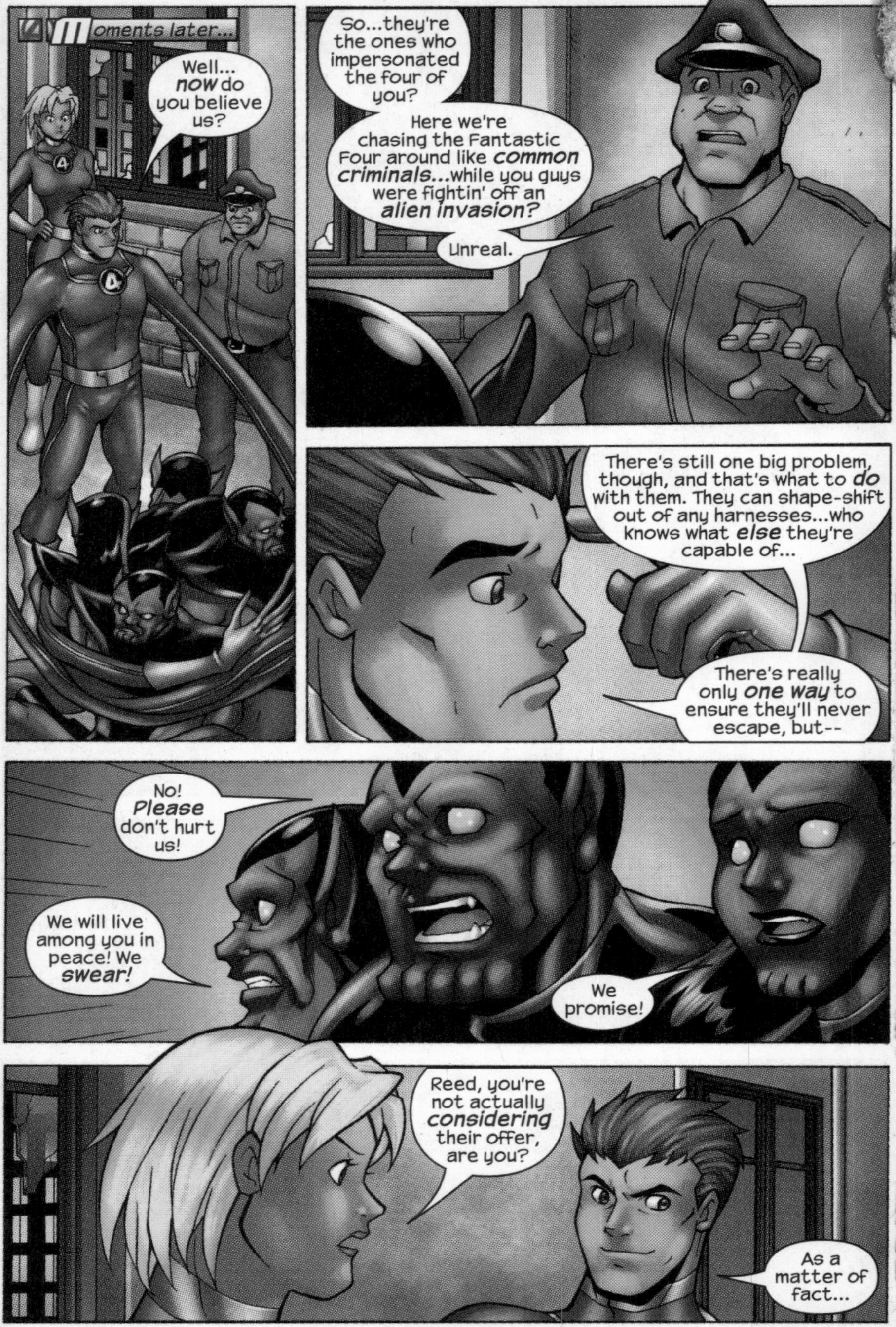
Moments later...
Well... *now* do you believe us?
So...they're the ones who impersonated the four of you?
Here we're chasing the Fantastic Four around like *common criminals*...while you guys were fightin' off an *alien invasion?*
Unreal.
There's still one big problem, though, and that's what to *do* with them. They can shape-shift out of any harnesses...who knows what *else* they're capable of...
There's really only *one way* to ensure they'll never escape, but--
No! *Please* don't hurt us!
We will live among you in peace! We *swear!*
We promise!
Reed, you're not actually *considering* their offer, are you?
As a matter of fact...

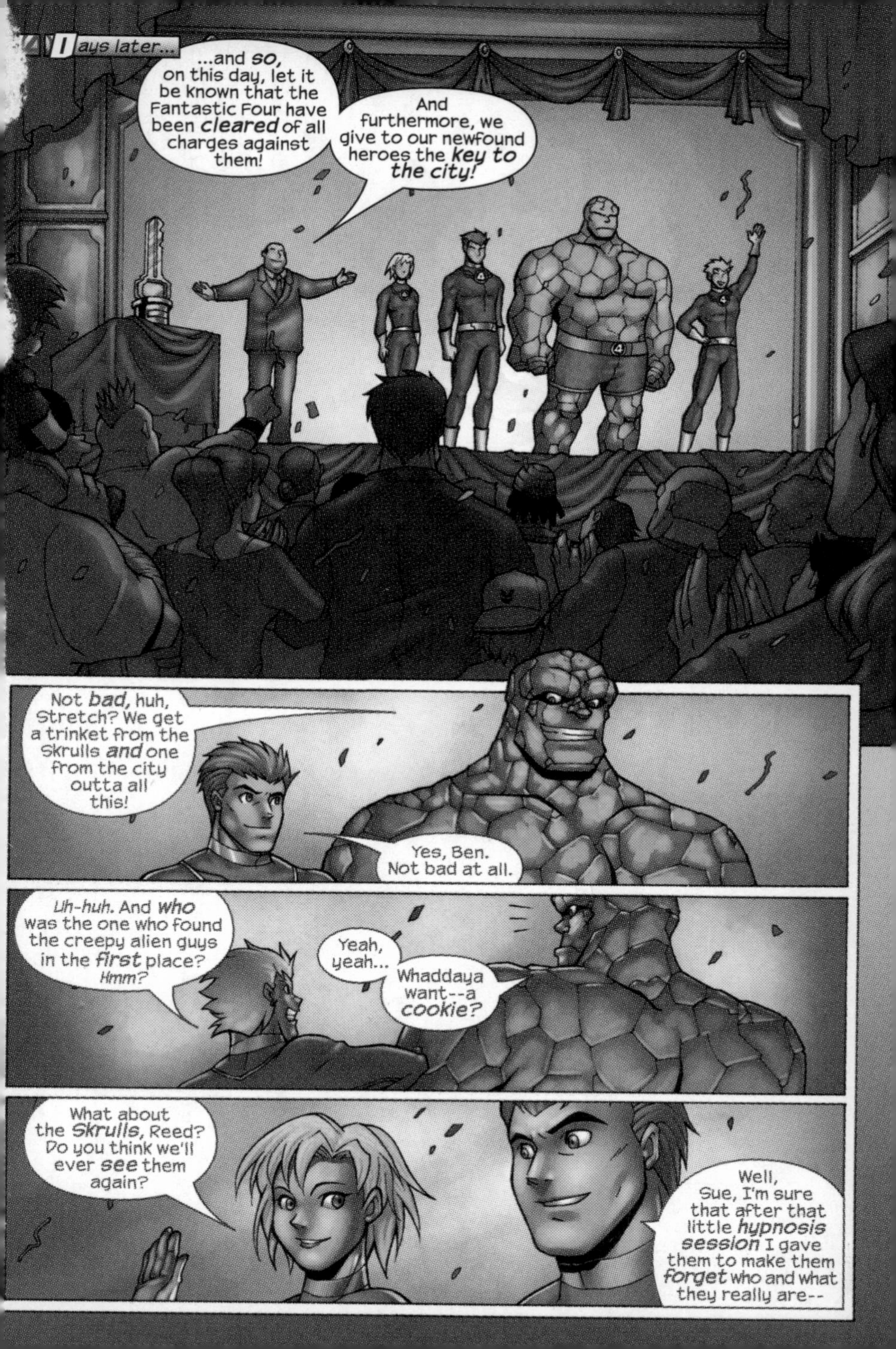
Days later...
...and so, on this day, let it be known that the Fantastic Four have been cleared of all charges against them!
And furthermore, we give to our newfound heroes the key to the city!
Not bad, huh, Stretch? We get a trinket from the Skrulls and one from the city outta all this!
Yes, Ben. Not bad at all.
Uh-huh. And who was the one who found the creepy alien guys in the first place? Hmm?
Yeah, yeah...
Whaddaya want--a cookie?
What about the Skrulls, Reed? Do you think we'll ever see them again?
Well, Sue, I'm sure that after that little hypnosis session I gave them to make them forget who and what they really are--

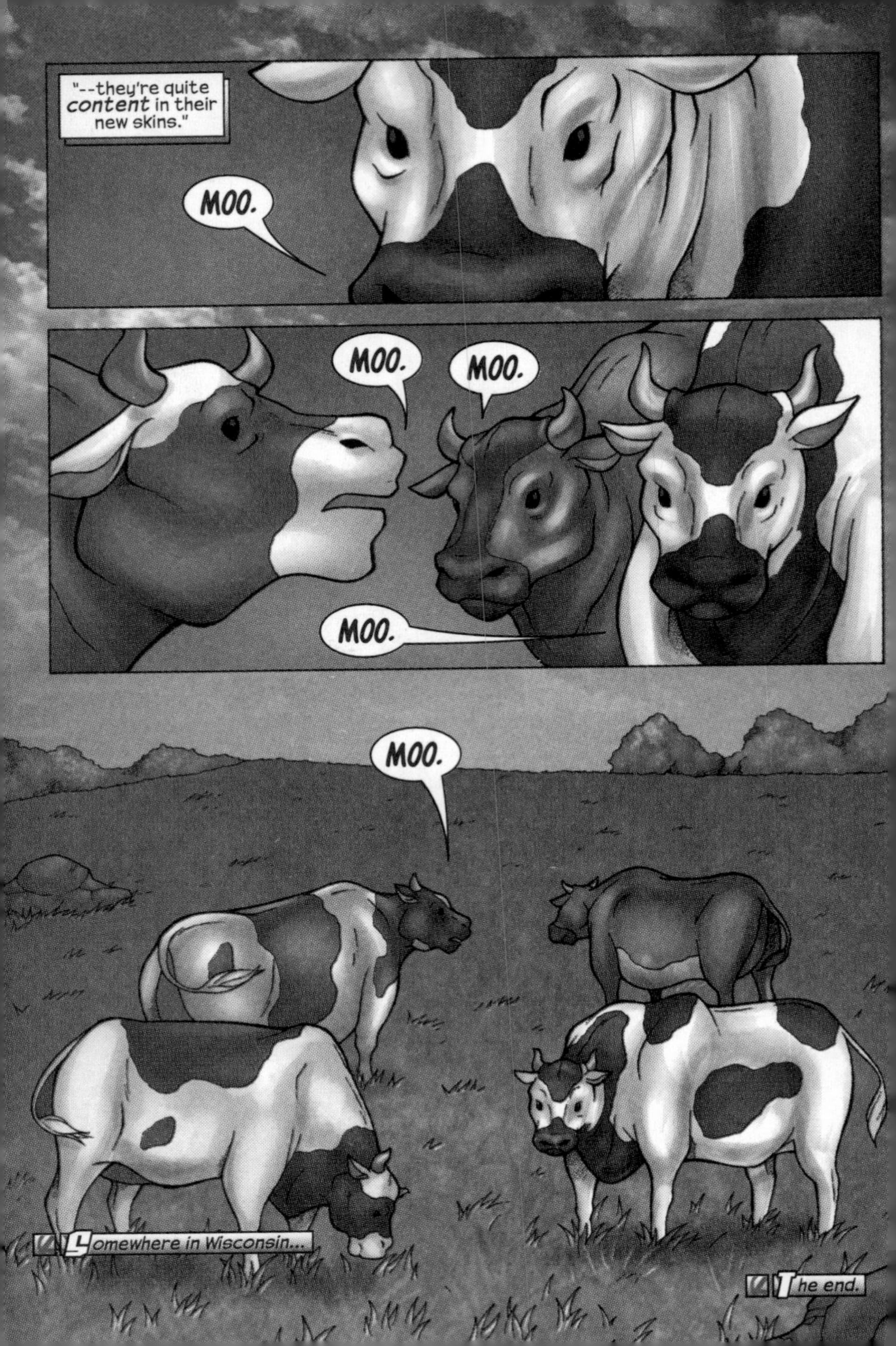
"--they're quite content in their new skins."
MOO.
MOO.
MOO.
MOO.
MOO.
Somewhere in Wisconsin...
The end.

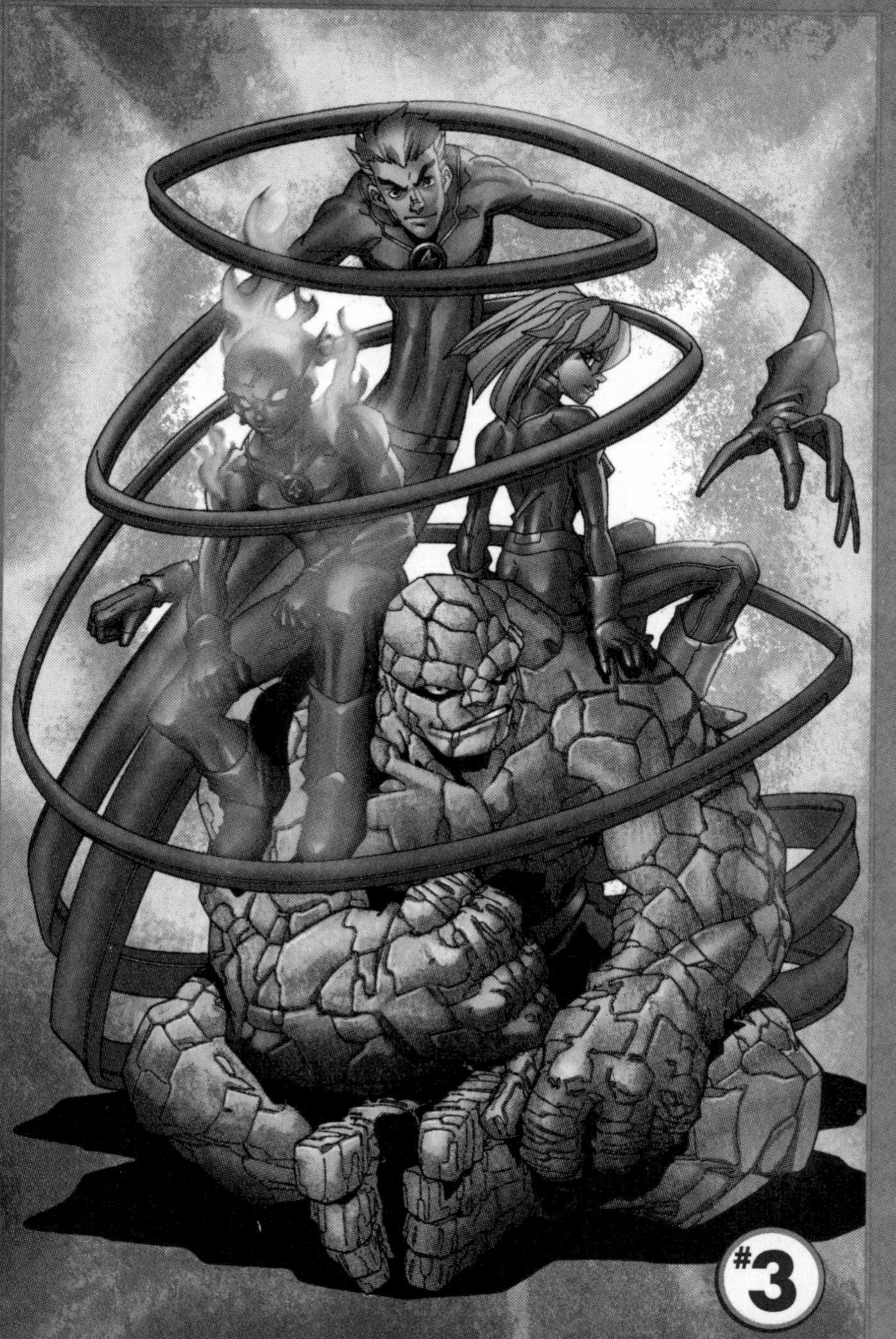
#3

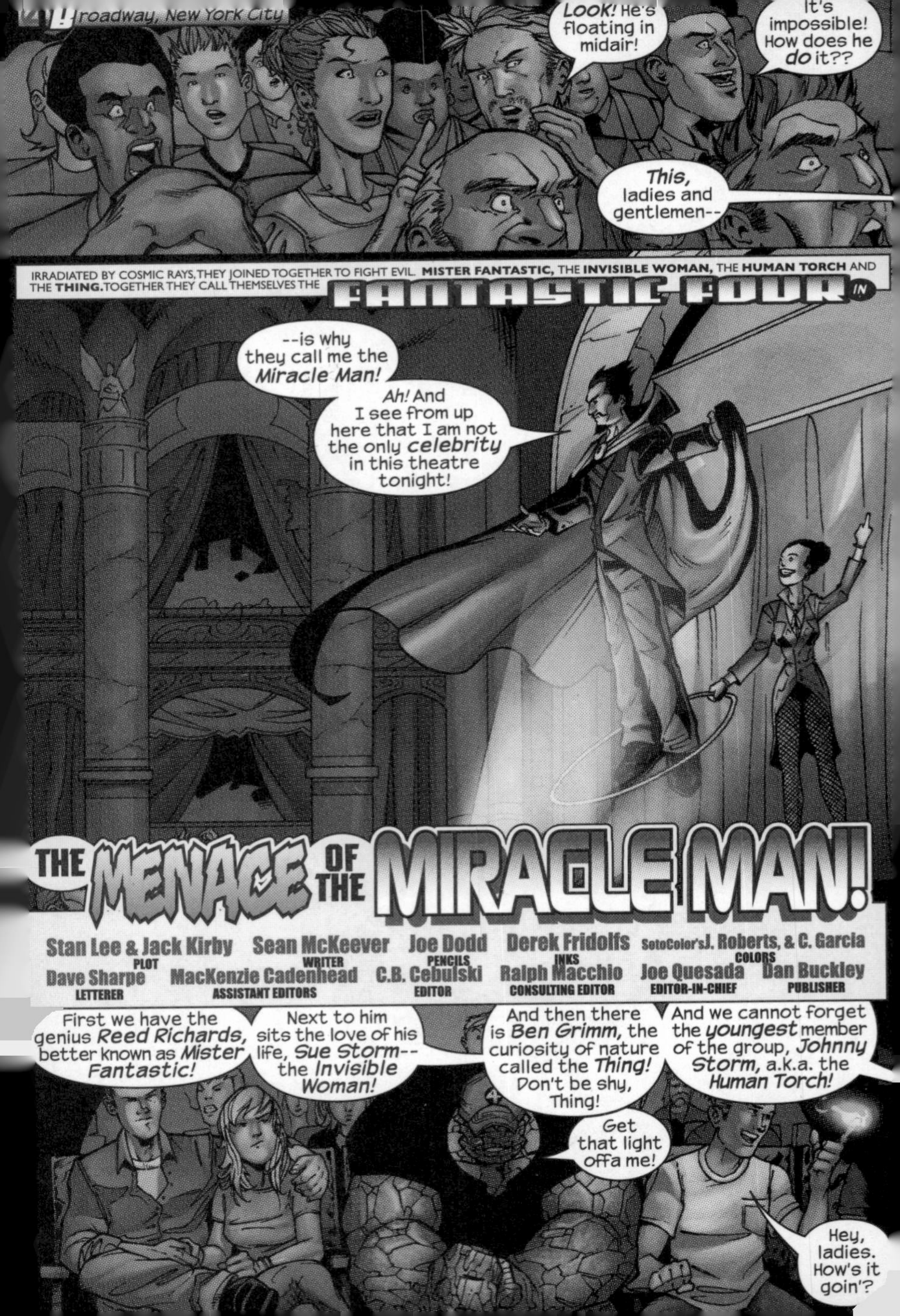

Broadway, New York City
LOOK! He's floating in midair!
It's impossible! How does he do it??
This, ladies and gentlemen--
IRRADIATED BY COSMIC RAYS, THEY JOINED TOGETHER TO FIGHT EVIL. MISTER FANTASTIC, THE INVISIBLE WOMAN, THE HUMAN TORCH AND THE THING. TOGETHER THEY CALL THEMSELVES THE FANTASTIC FOUR IN
--is why they call me the Miracle Man!
Ah! And I see from up here that I am not the only celebrity in this theatre tonight!
THE MENACE OF THE MIRACLE MAN!
Stan Lee & Jack Kirby PLOT
Sean McKeever WRITER
Joe Dodd PENCILS
Derek Fridolfs INKS
SotoColor's J. Roberts, & C. Garcia COLORS
Dave Sharpe LETTERER
MacKenzie Cadenhead C.B. Cebulski ASSISTANT EDITORS
Ralph Macchio EDITOR
Joe Quesada CONSULTING EDITOR
Dan Buckley EDITOR-IN-CHIEF PUBLISHER
First we have the genius Reed Richards, better known as Mister Fantastic!
Next to him sits the love of his life, Sue Storm-- the Invisible Woman!
And then there is Ben Grimm, the curiosity of nature called the Thing! Don't be shy, Thing!
Get that light offa me!
And we cannot forget the youngest member of the group, Johnny Storm, a.k.a. the Human Torch!
Hey, ladies. How's it goin'?

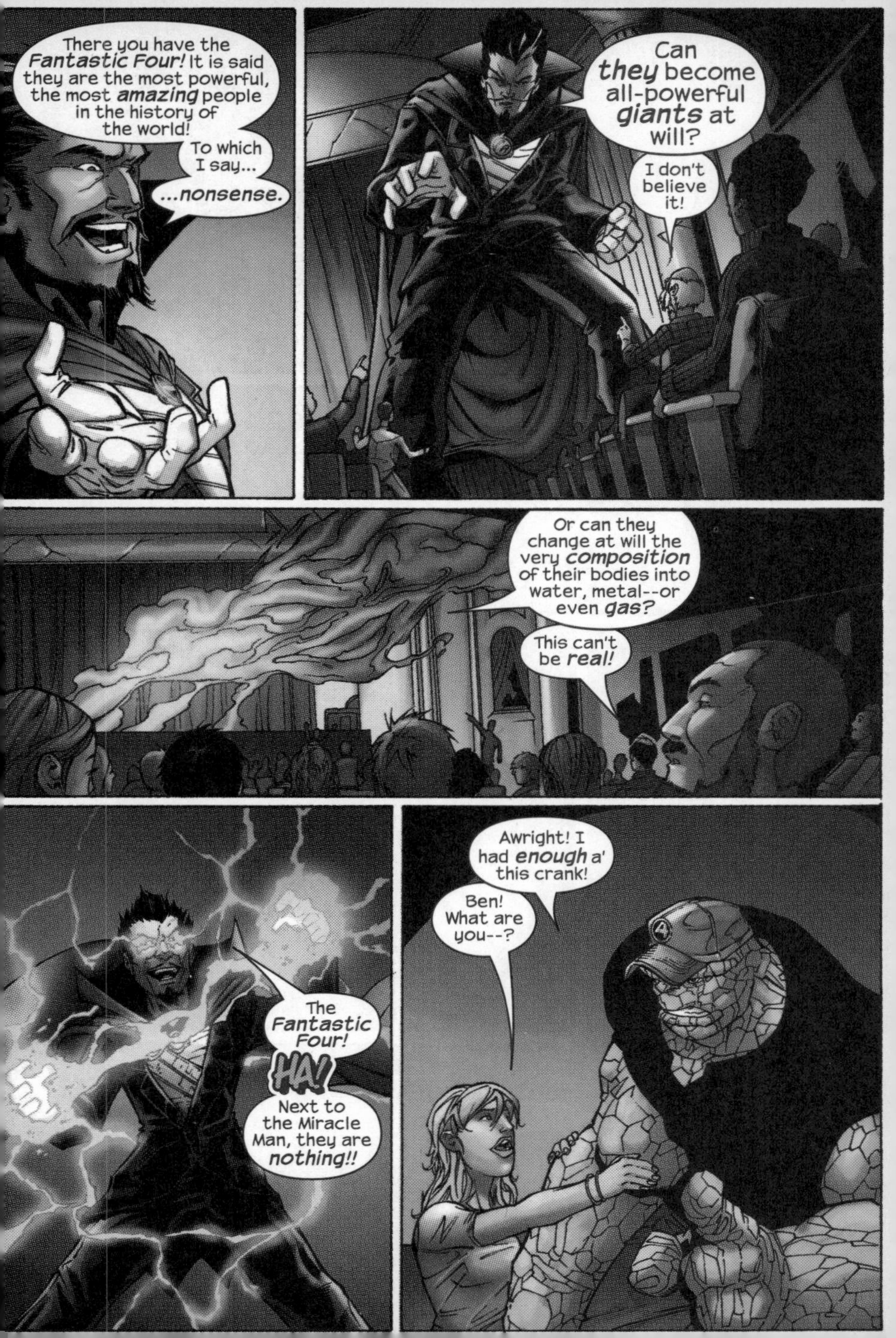
There you have the Fantastic Four! It is said they are the most powerful, the most amazing people in the history of the world!
To which I say...
...nonsense.
Can they become all-powerful giants at will?
I don't believe it!
Or can they change at will the very composition of their bodies into water, metal--or even gas?
This can't be real!
The Fantastic Four!
HA!
Next to the Miracle Man, they are nothing!!
Awright! I had enough a' this crank!
Ben! What are you--?

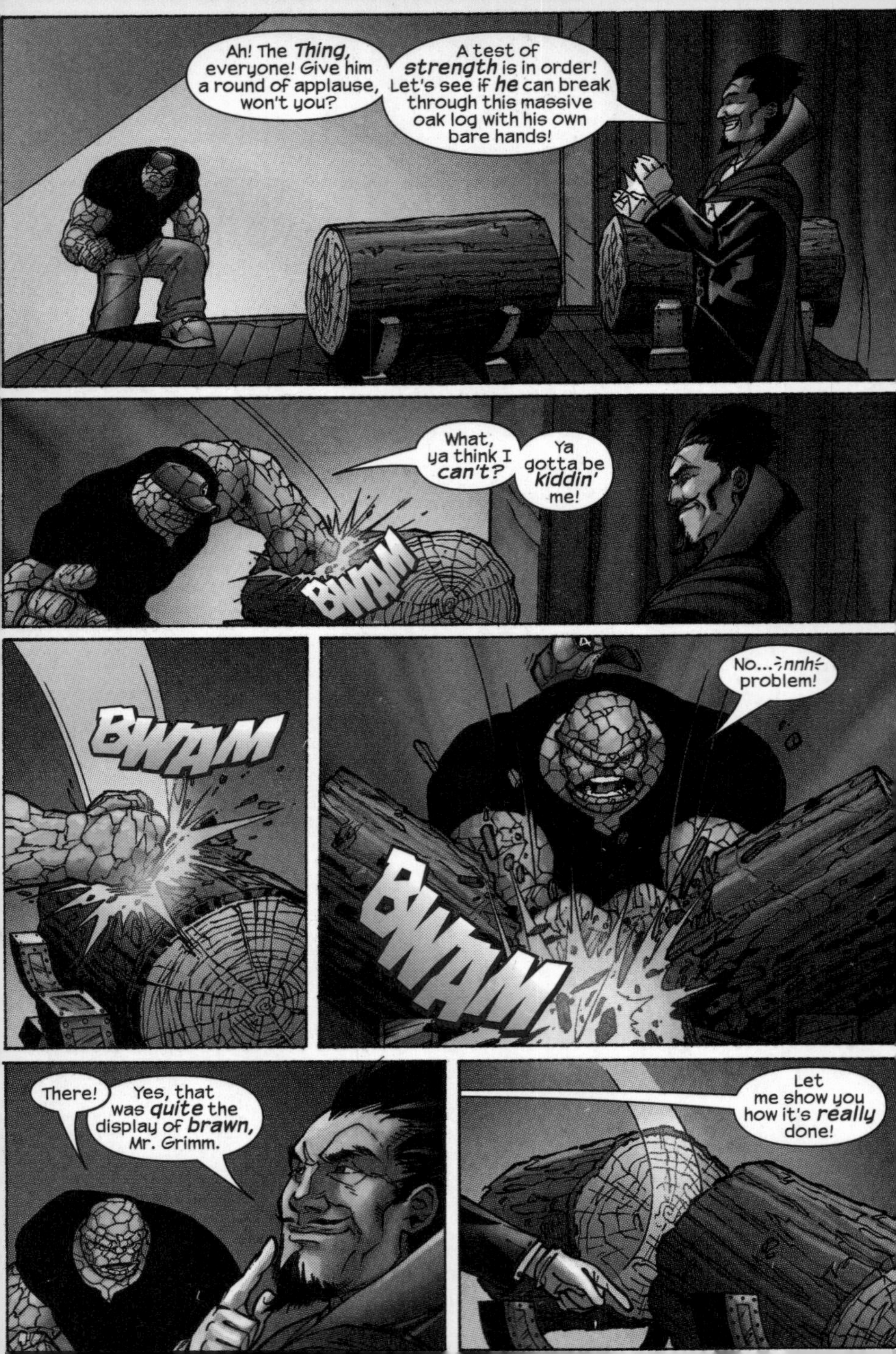
Ah! The *Thing*, everyone! Give him a round of applause, won't you?
A test of *strength* is in order! Let's see if *he* can break through this massive oak log with his own bare hands!
What, ya think I *can't*?
Ya gotta be *kiddin'* me!
BWAM
BWAM
No...=nnh= problem!
BWAM
There!
Yes, that was *quite* the display of *brawn*, Mr. Grimm.
Let me show you how it's *really* done!

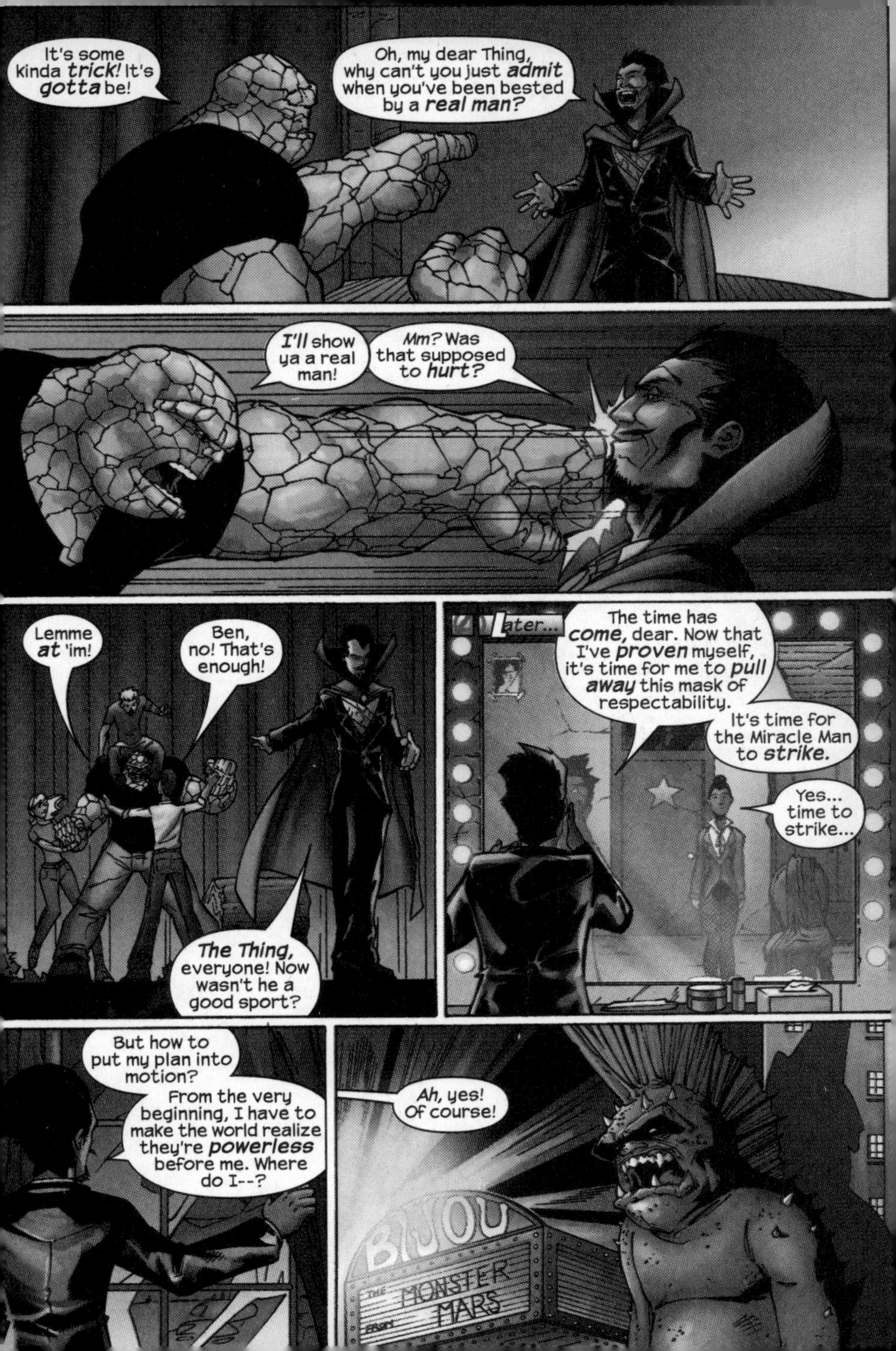
It's some kinda trick! It's gotta be!
Oh, my dear Thing, why can't you just admit when you've been bested by a real man?
I'll show ya a real man!
Mm? Was that supposed to hurt?
Lemme at 'im!
Ben, no! That's enough!
The Thing, everyone! Now wasn't he a good sport?
Later...
The time has come, dear. Now that I've proven myself, it's time for me to pull away this mask of respectability.
It's time for the Miracle Man to strike.
Yes... time to strike...
But how to put my plan into motion?
From the very beginning, I have to make the world realize they're powerless before me. Where do I--?
Ah, yes! Of course!
BIJOU
THE MONSTER
MARS

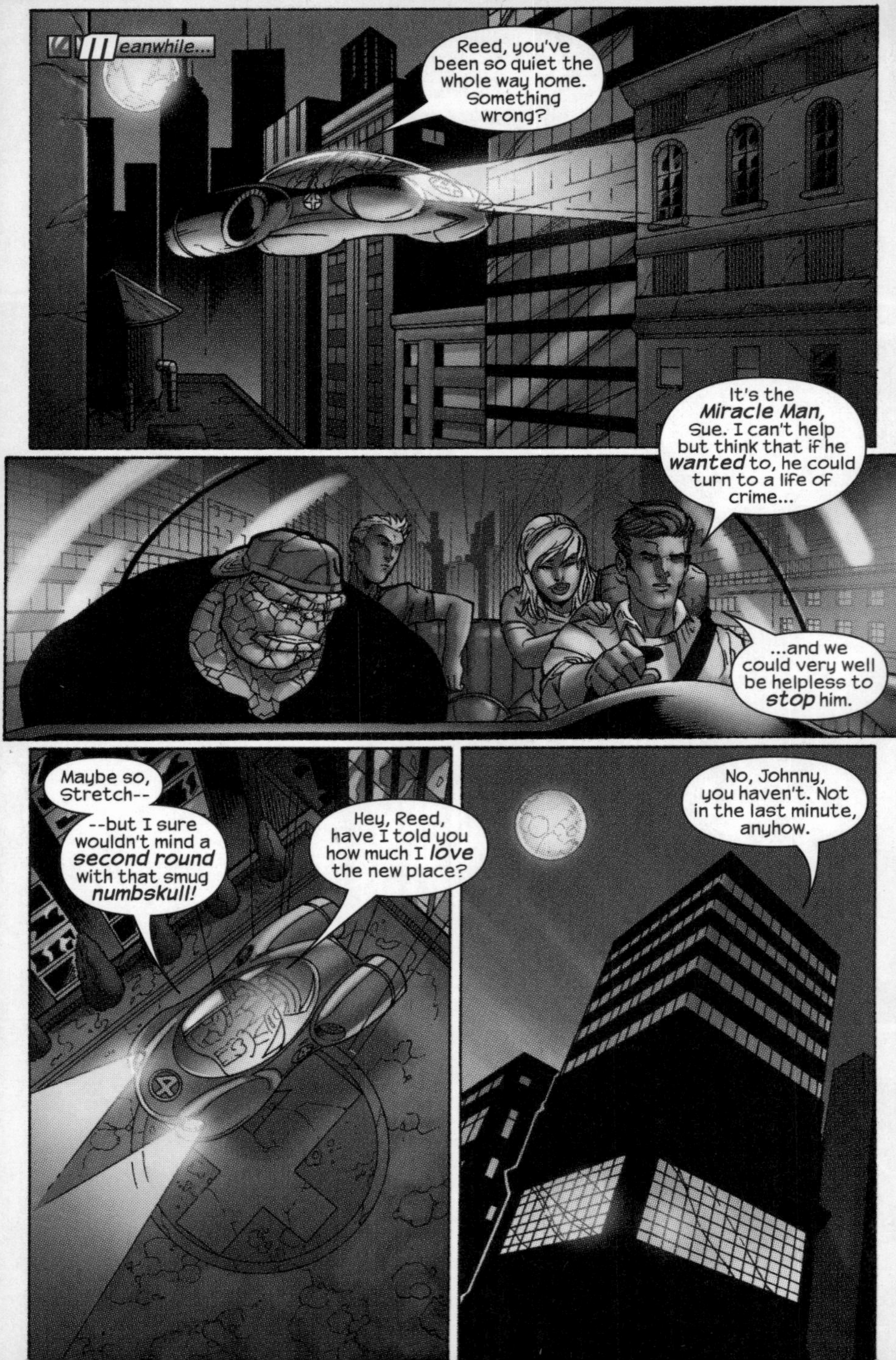
Meanwhile...
Reed, you've been so quiet the whole way home. Something wrong?
It's the Miracle Man, Sue. I can't help but think that if he wanted to, he could turn to a life of crime...
...and we could very well be helpless to stop him.
Maybe so, Stretch--
--but I sure wouldn't mind a second round with that smug numbskull!
Hey, Reed, have I told you how much I love the new place?
No, Johnny, you haven't. Not in the last minute, anyhow.

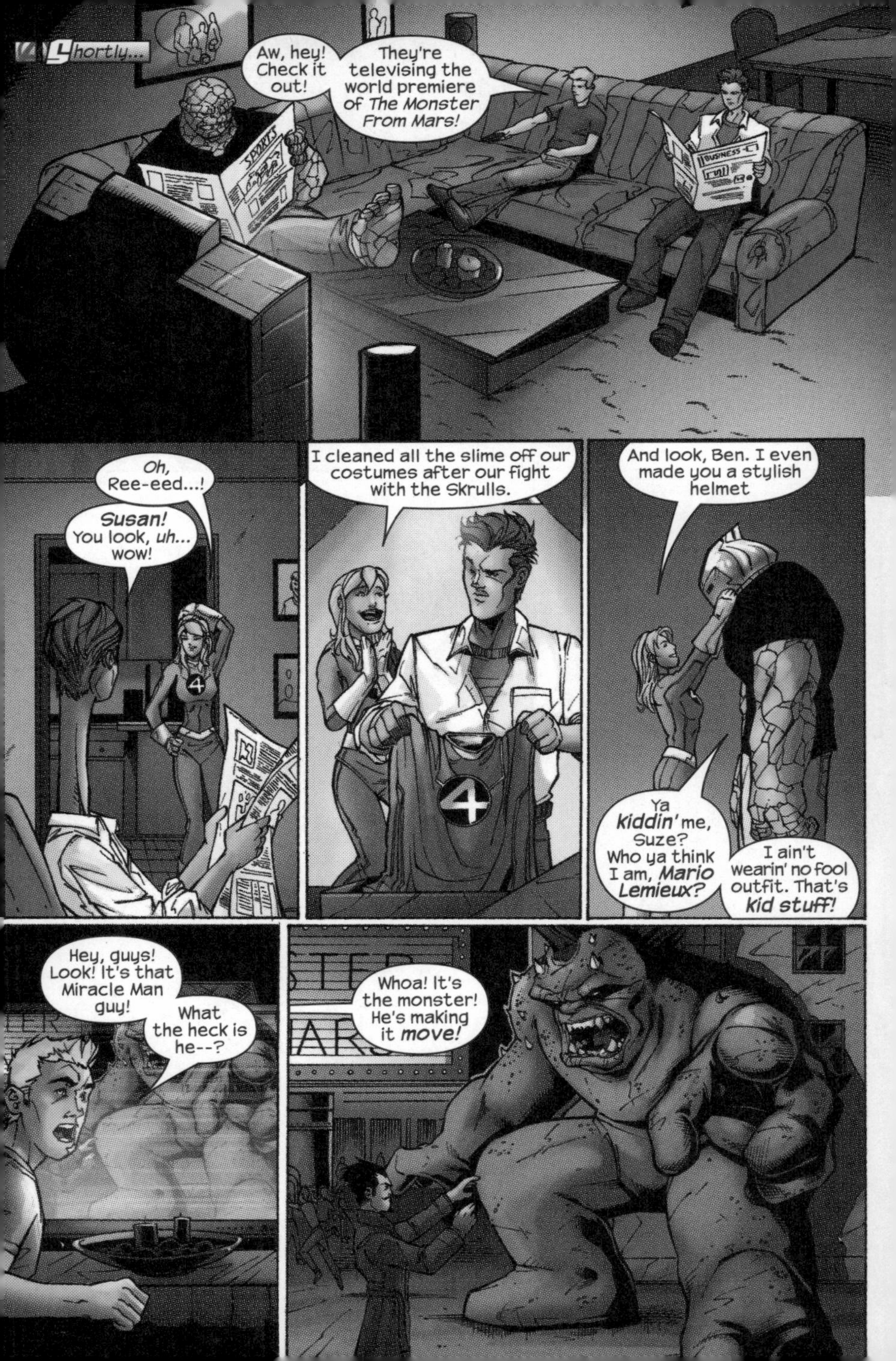
Shortly...
Aw, hey! Check it out!
They're televising the world premiere of *The Monster From Mars!*
Oh, Ree-eed...!
*Susan!* You look, *uh...* wow!
I cleaned all the slime off our costumes after our fight with the Skrulls.
And look, Ben. I even made you a stylish helmet
Ya *kiddin'* me, Suze? Who ya think I am, *Mario Lemieux?*
I ain't wearin' no fool outfit. That's *kid stuff!*
Hey, guys! Look! It's that Miracle Man guy!
What the heck is he--?
Whoa! It's the monster! He's making it *move!*

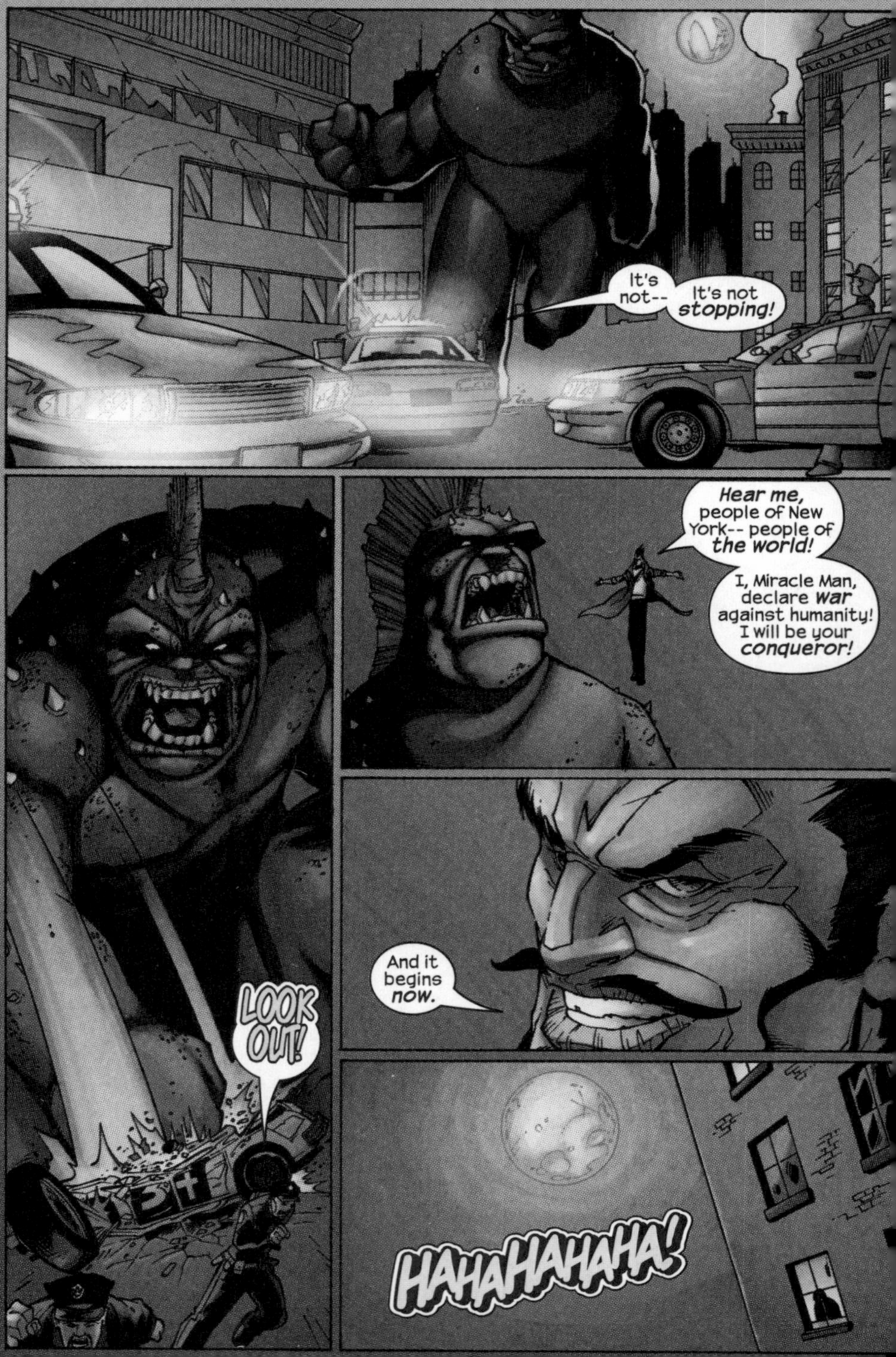
It's not--
It's not stopping!
Hear me, people of New York-- people of the world!
I, Miracle Man, declare war against humanity! I will be your conqueror!
And it begins now.
LOOK OUT!
HAHAHAHAHA!

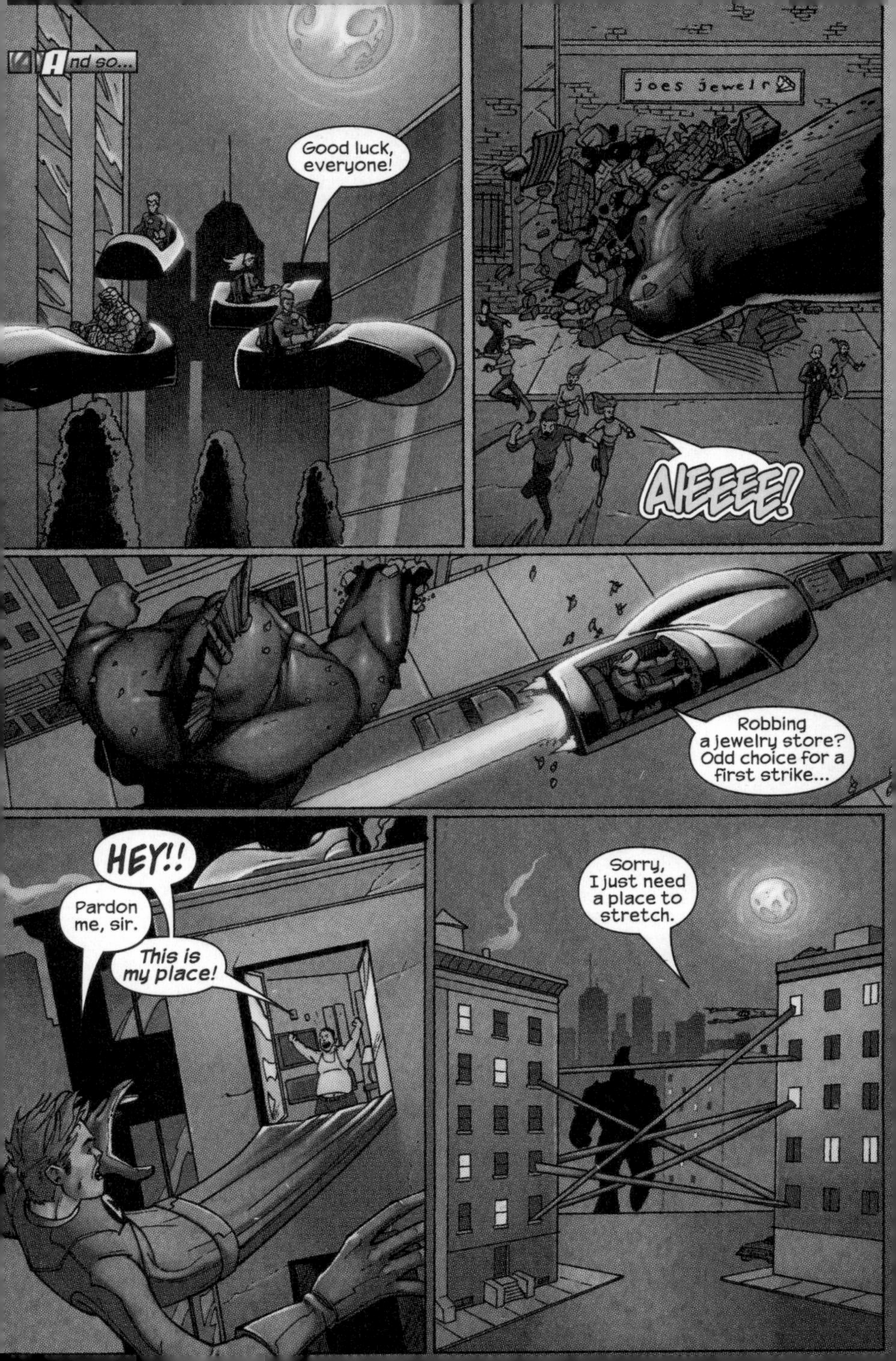
And so...
Good luck, everyone!
joes jewelry
AIEEEE!
Robbing a jewelry store? Odd choice for a first strike...
HEY!!
Pardon me, sir.
This is my place!
Sorry, I just need a place to stretch.

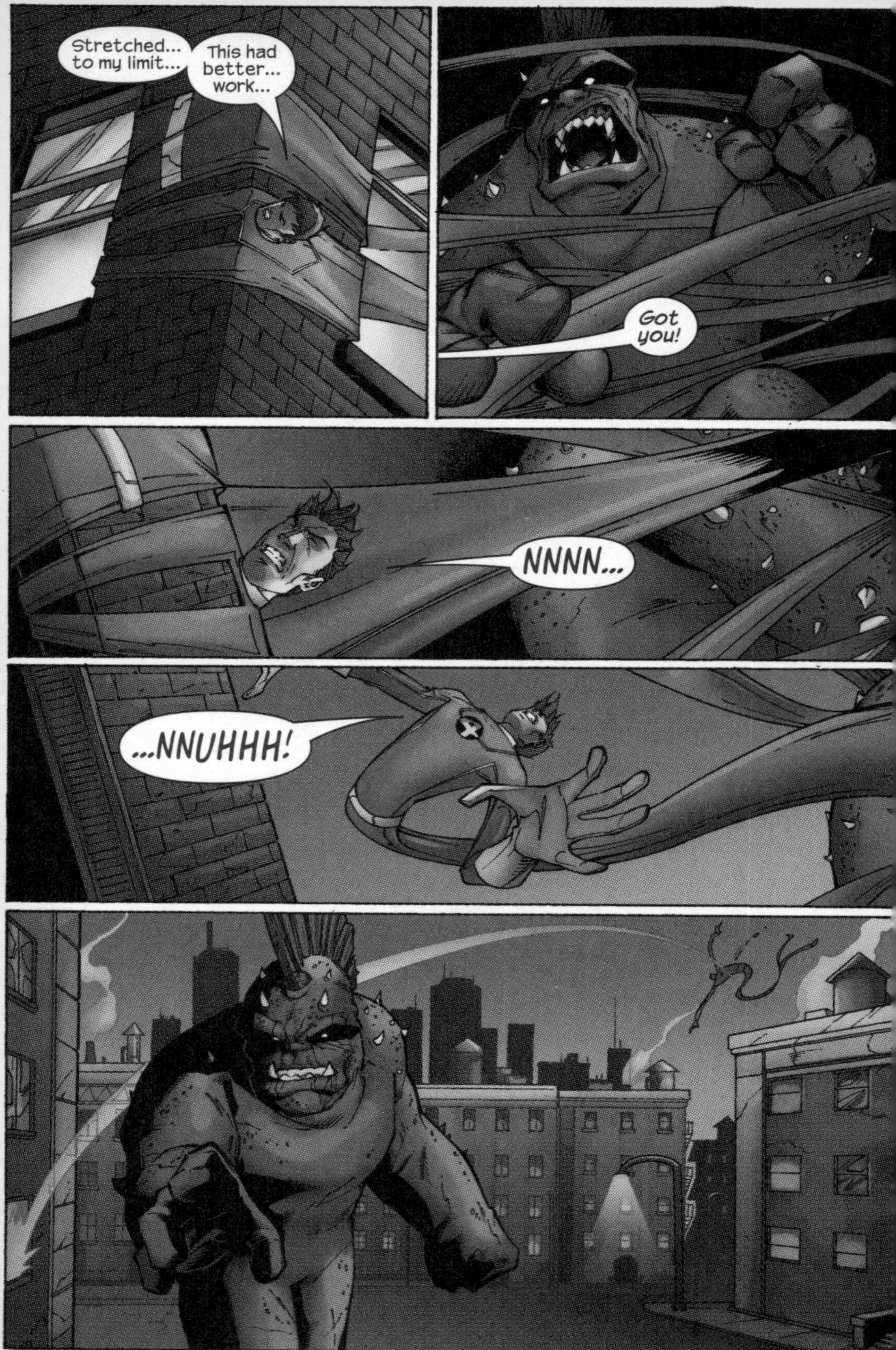
Stretched... to my limit...
This had better... work...
Got you!
NNNN...
...NNUHHH!

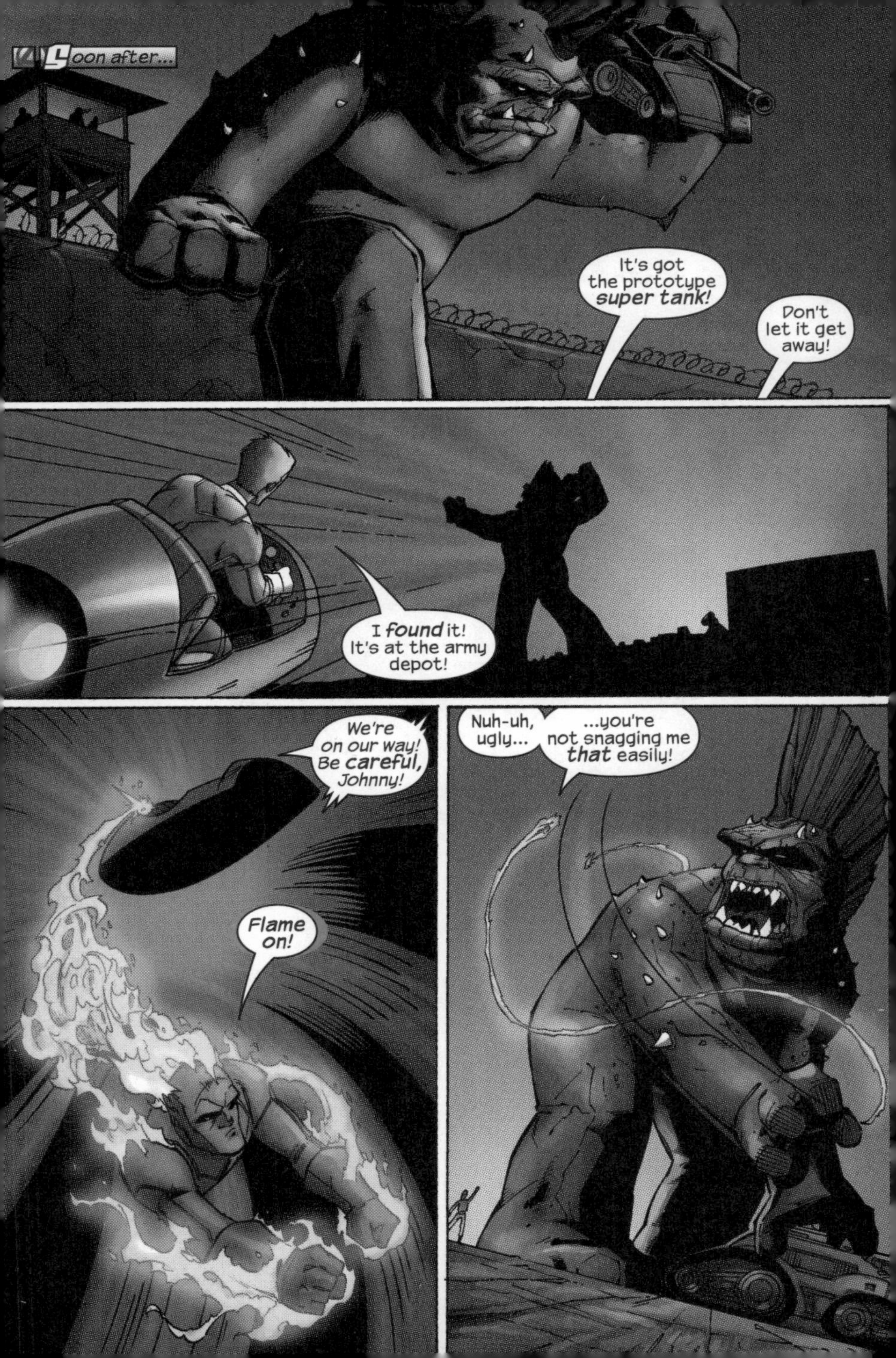
Soon after...
It's got the prototype super tank!
Don't let it get away!
I found it! It's at the army depot!
We're on our way! Be careful, Johnny!
Flame on!
Nuh-uh, ugly...
...you're not snagging me that easily!

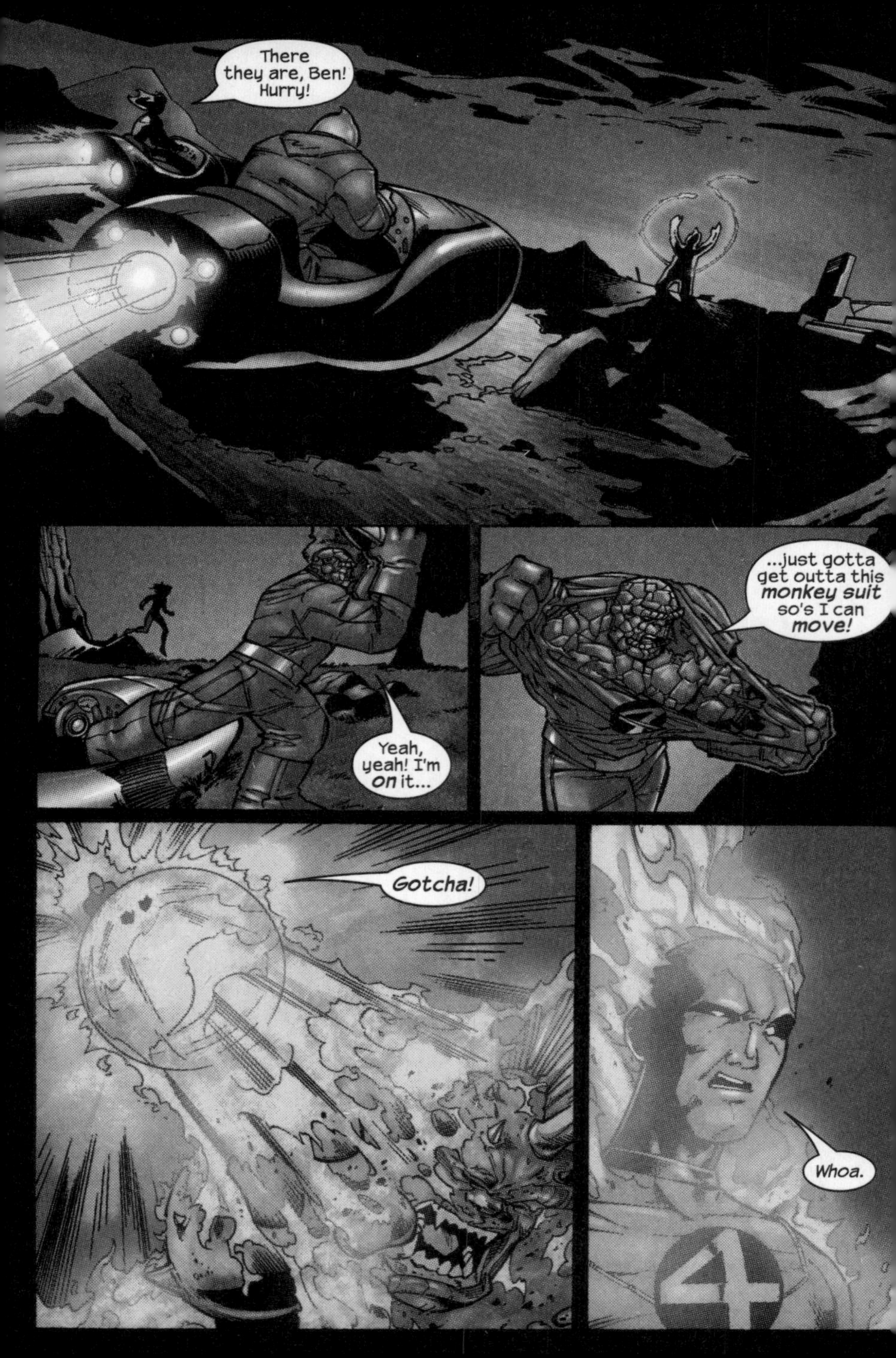
There they are, Ben! Hurry!
Yeah, yeah! I'm on it...
...just gotta get outta this monkey suit so's I can move!
Gotcha!
Whoa.

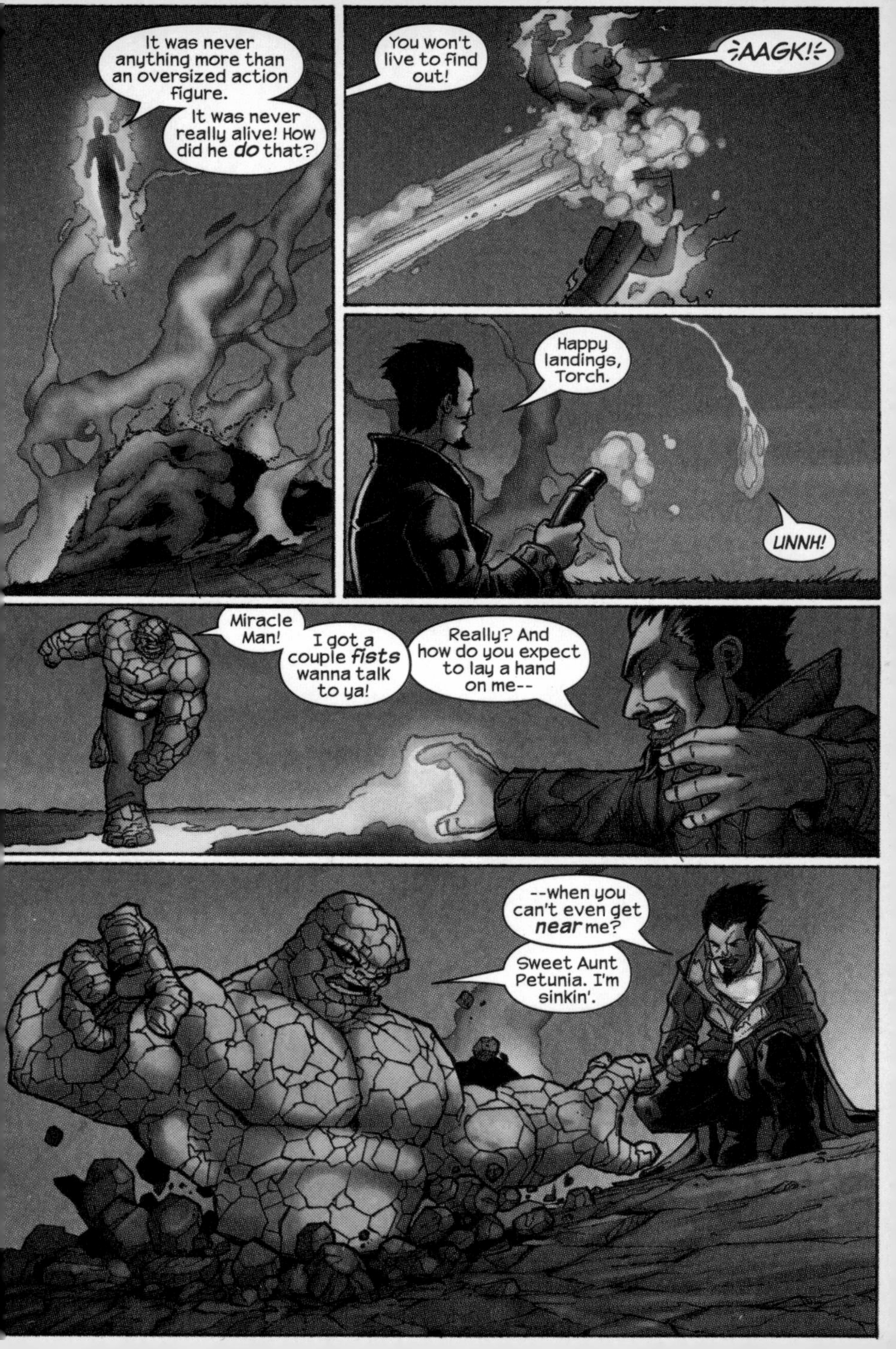
It was never anything more than an oversized action figure.
It was never really alive! How did he *do* that?
You won't live to find out!
AAGK!!
Happy landings, Torch.
UNNH!
Miracle Man!
I got a couple *fists* wanna talk to ya!
Really? And how do you expect to lay a hand on me--
--when you can't even get *near* me?
Sweet Aunt Petunia. I'm sinkin'.

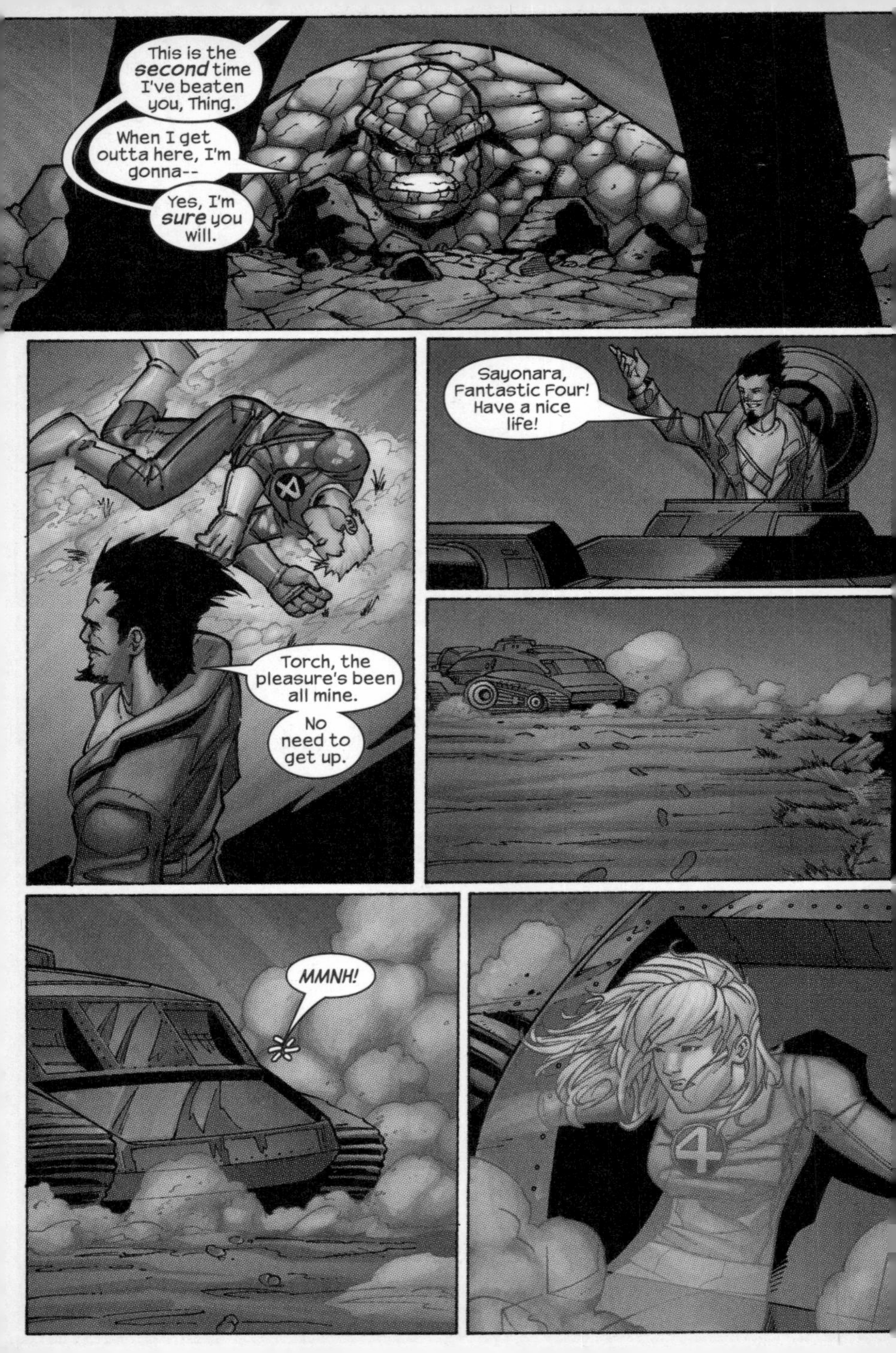
This is the *second* time I've beaten you, Thing.
When I get outta here, I'm gonna--
Yes, I'm *sure* you will.
Torch, the pleasure's been all mine.
No need to get up.
Sayonara, Fantastic Four! Have a nice life!
MMNH!

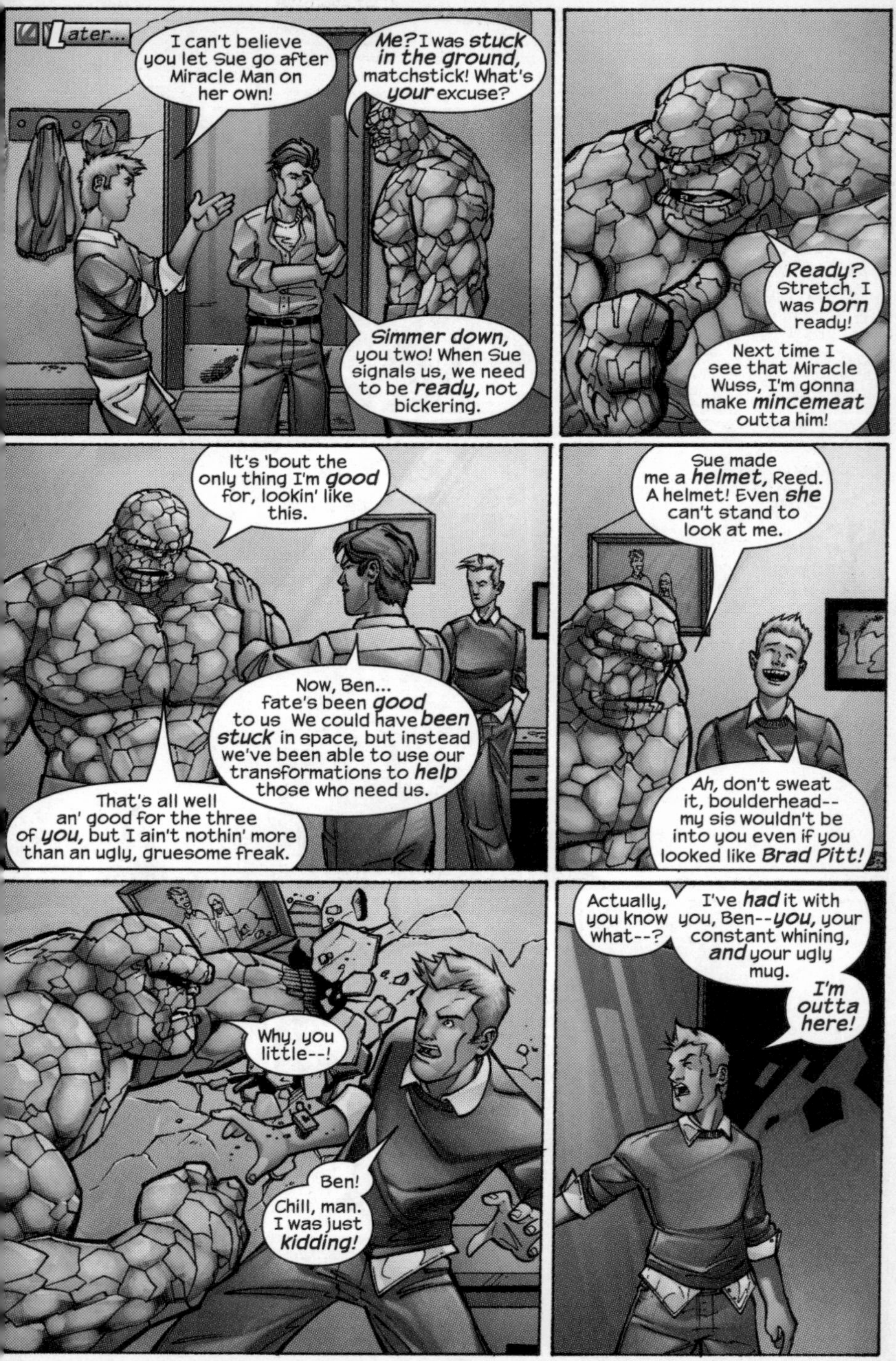
Later...
I can't believe you let Sue go after Miracle Man on her own!
Me? I was stuck in the ground, matchstick! What's your excuse?
Simmer down, you two! When Sue signals us, we need to be ready, not bickering.
Ready? Stretch, I was born ready!
Next time I see that Miracle Wuss, I'm gonna make mincemeat outta him!
It's 'bout the only thing I'm good for, lookin' like this.
Now, Ben... fate's been good to us We could have been stuck in space, but instead we've been able to use our transformations to help those who need us.
That's all well an' good for the three of you, but I ain't nothin' more than an ugly, gruesome freak.
Sue made me a helmet, Reed. A helmet! Even she can't stand to look at me.
Ah, don't sweat it, boulderhead-- my sis wouldn't be into you even if you looked like Brad Pitt!
Why, you little--!
Ben! Chill, man. I was just kidding!
Actually, you know what--?
I've had it with you, Ben--you, your constant whining, and your ugly mug.
I'm outta here!

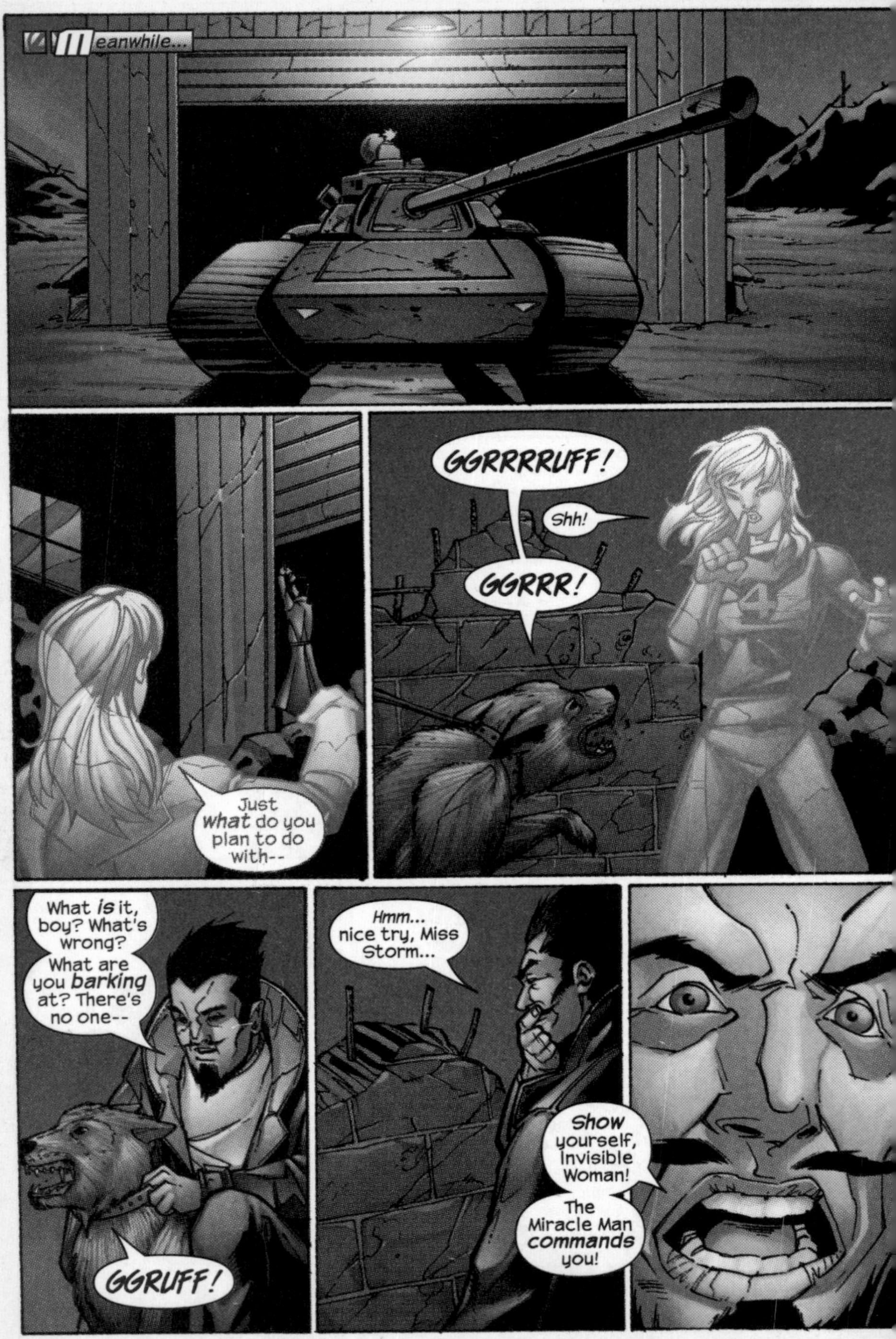
Meanwhile...
Just what do you plan to do with--
GGRRRRRUFF!
Shh!
GGRRR!
What is it, boy? What's wrong? What are you barking at? There's no one--
GGRUFF!
Hmm... nice try, Miss Storm...
Show yourself, Invisible Woman!
The Miracle Man commands you!

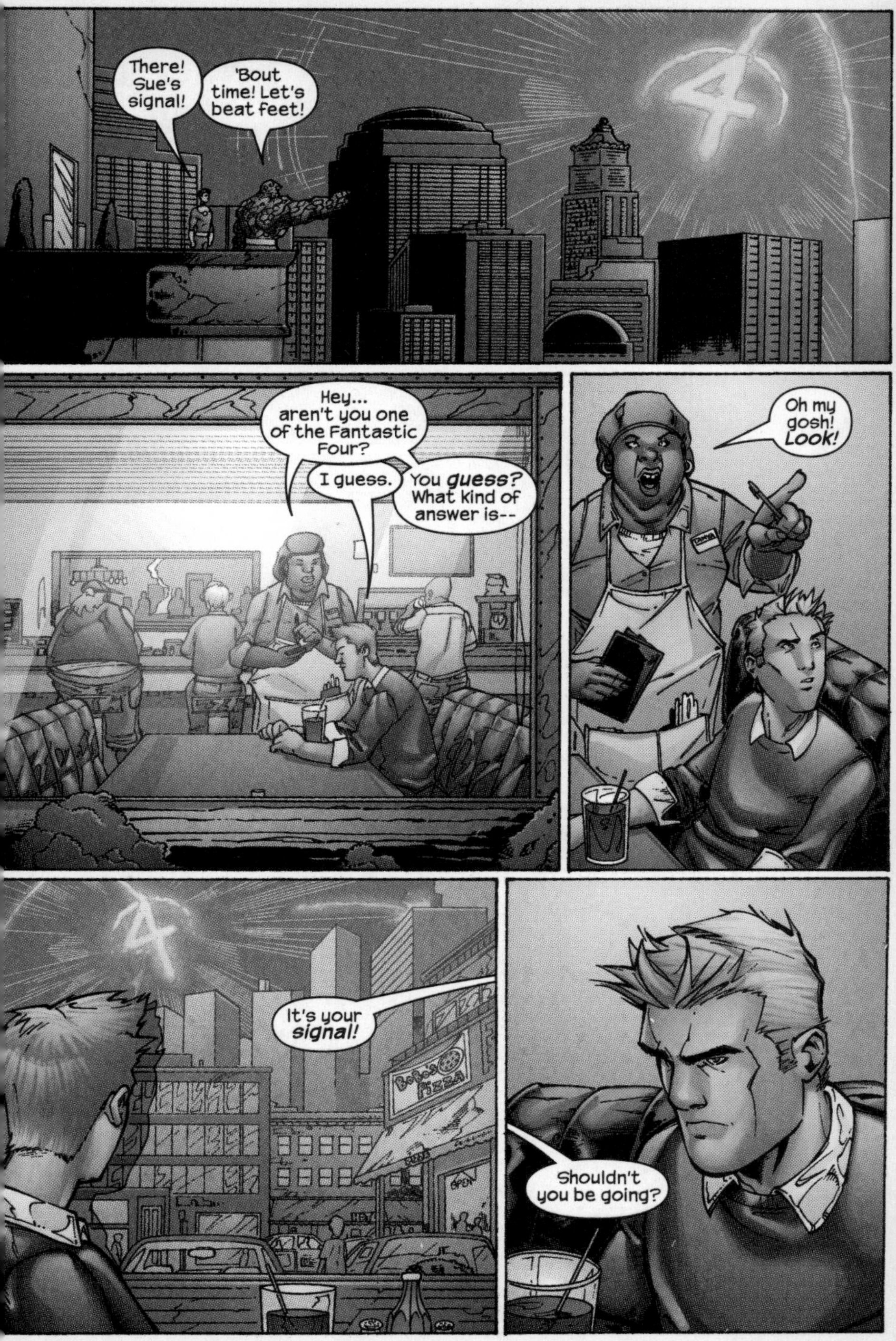
There! Sue's signal!
'Bout time! Let's beat feet!
Hey... aren't you one of the Fantastic Four?
I guess.
You *guess?* What kind of answer is--
Oh my gosh! *Look!*
It's your *signal!*
Shouldn't you be going?

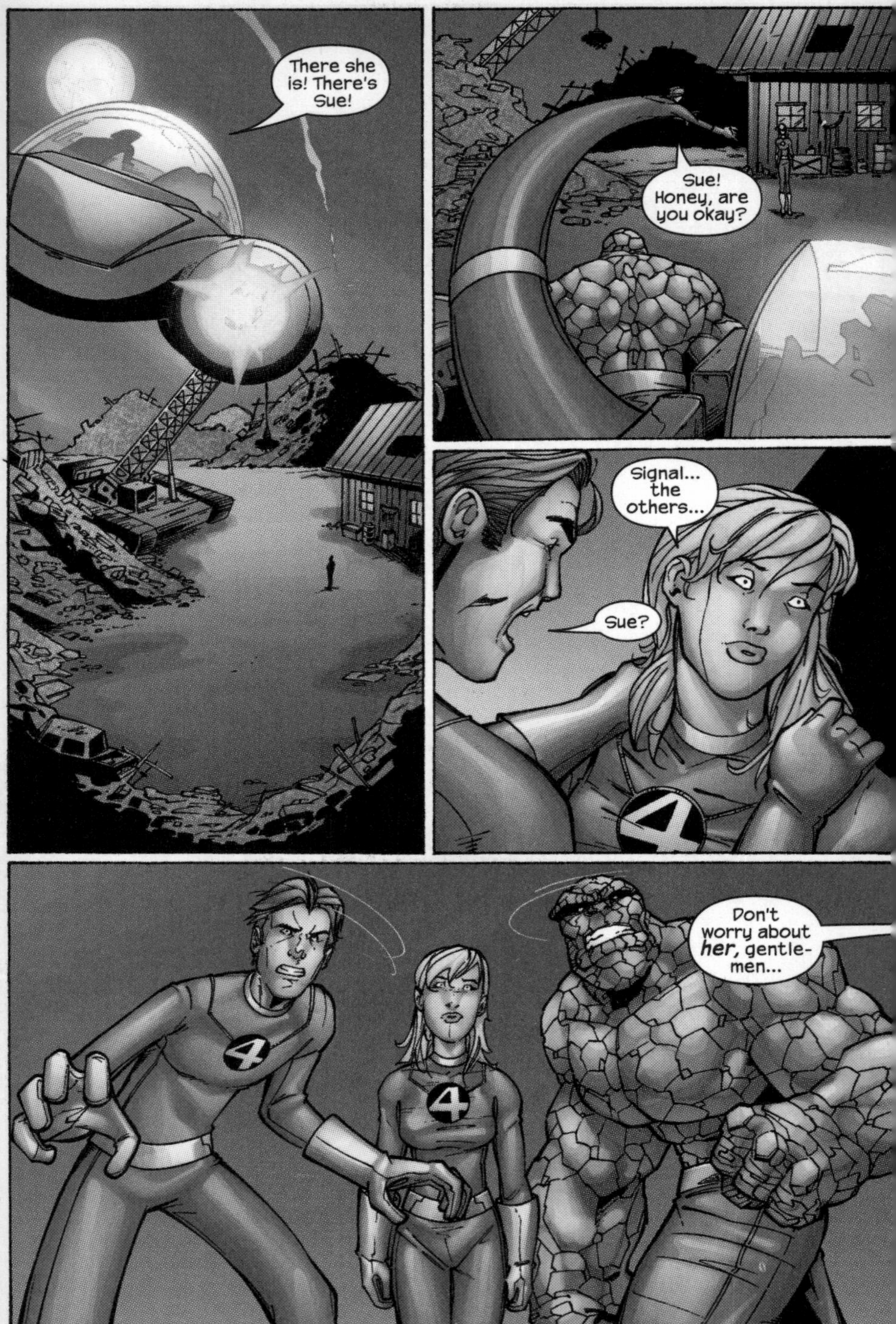
There she is! There's Sue!
Sue! Honey, are you okay?
Signal... the others...
Sue?
Don't worry about *her*, gentle-men...

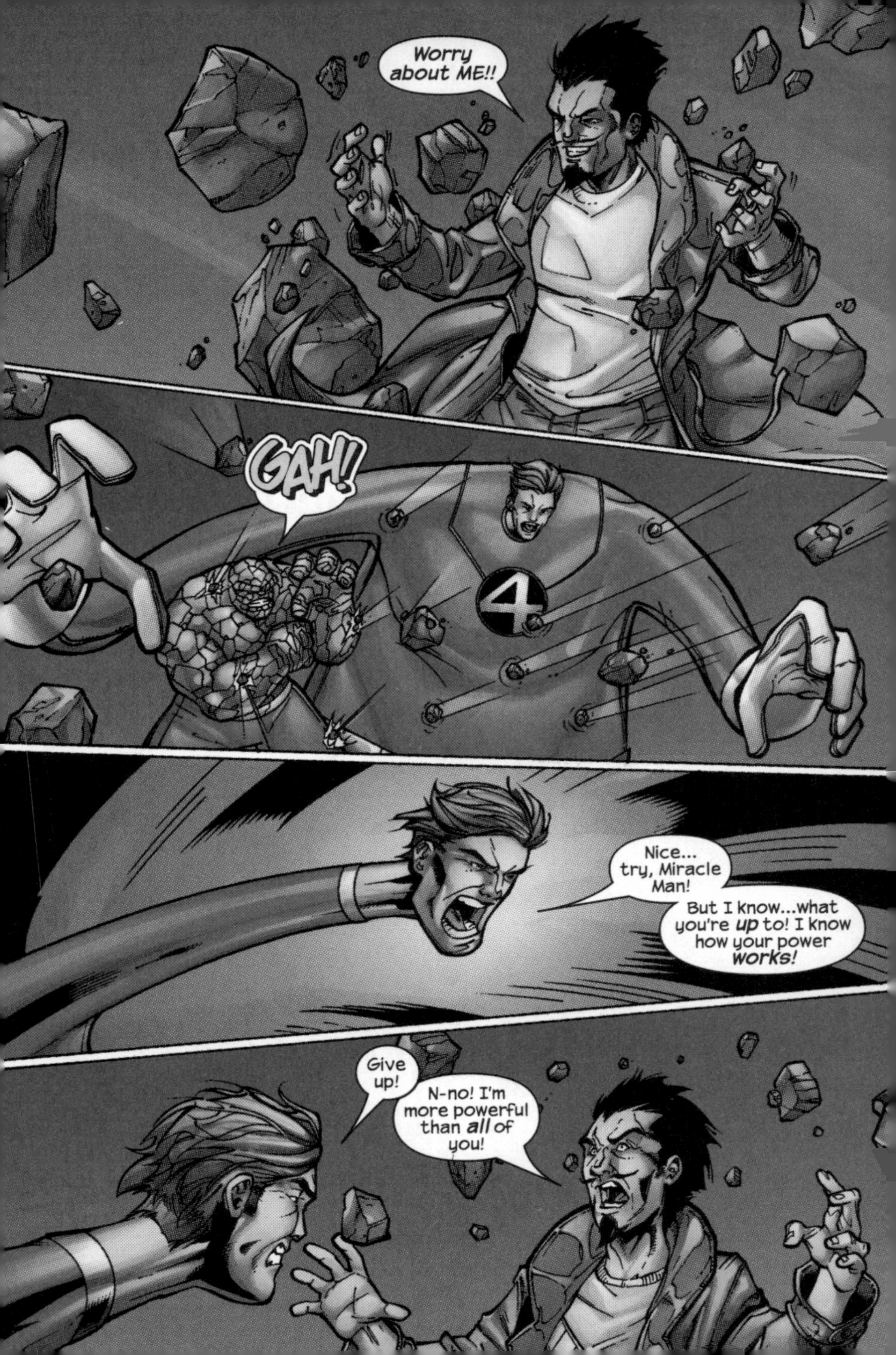
Worry about ME!!
GAH!!
Nice... try, Miracle Man!
But I know...what you're *up* to! I know how your power *works!*
Give up!
N-no! I'm more powerful than *all* of you!

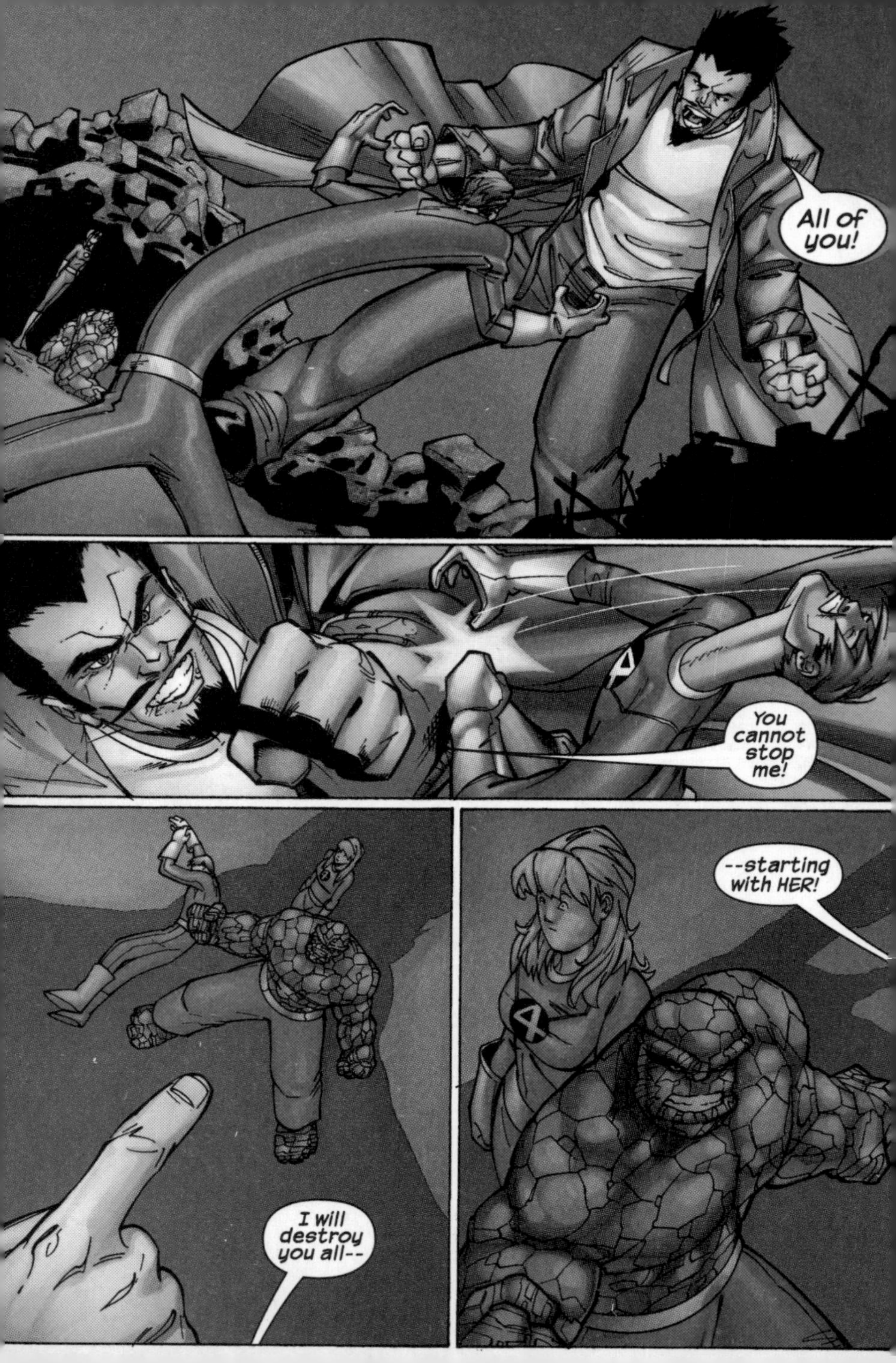
All of you!
You cannot stop me!
I will destroy you all--
--starting with HER!

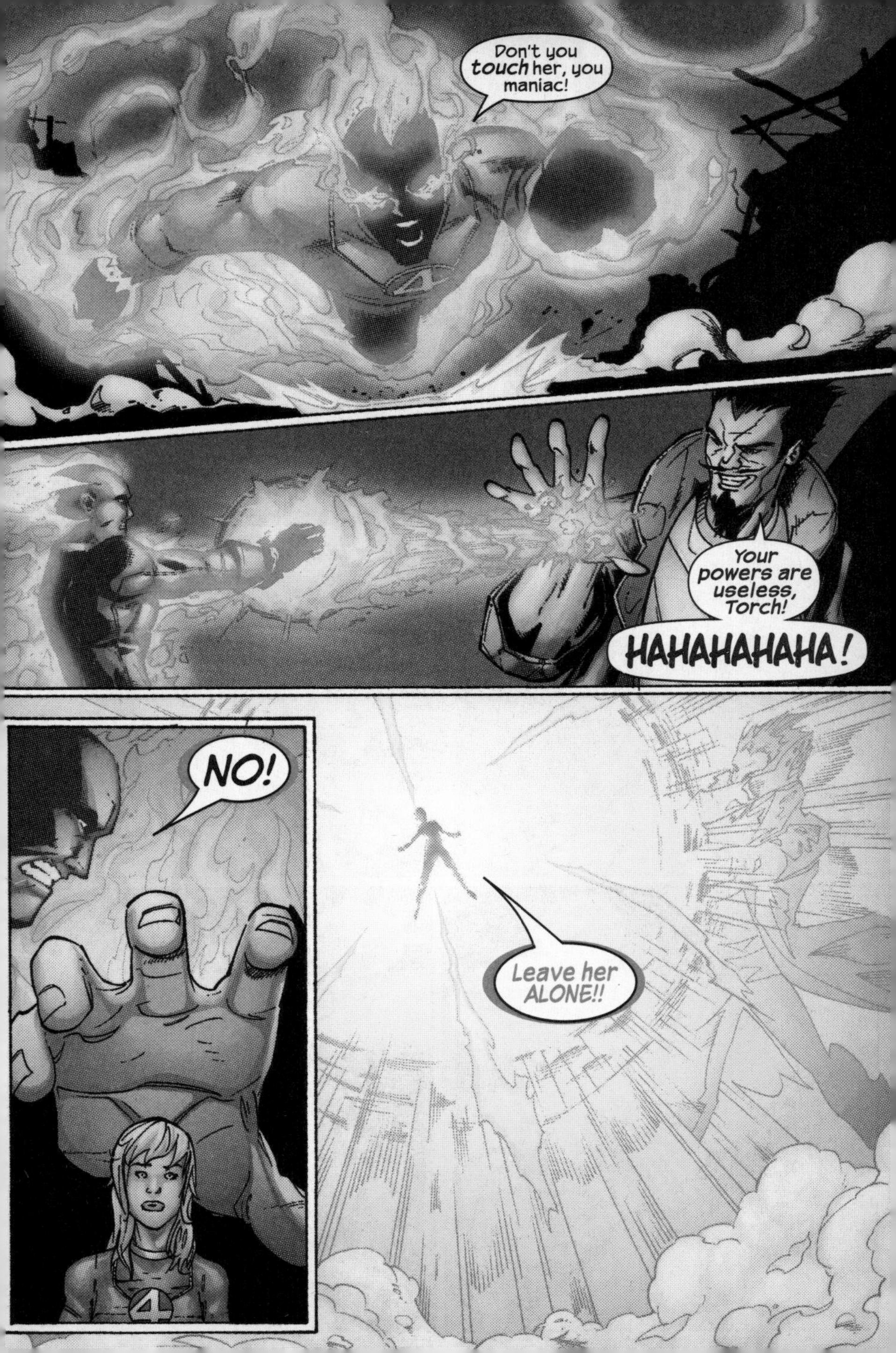
Don't you *touch* her, you maniac!
Your powers are useless, Torch!
HAHAHAHAHA!
NO!
Leave her ALONE!!

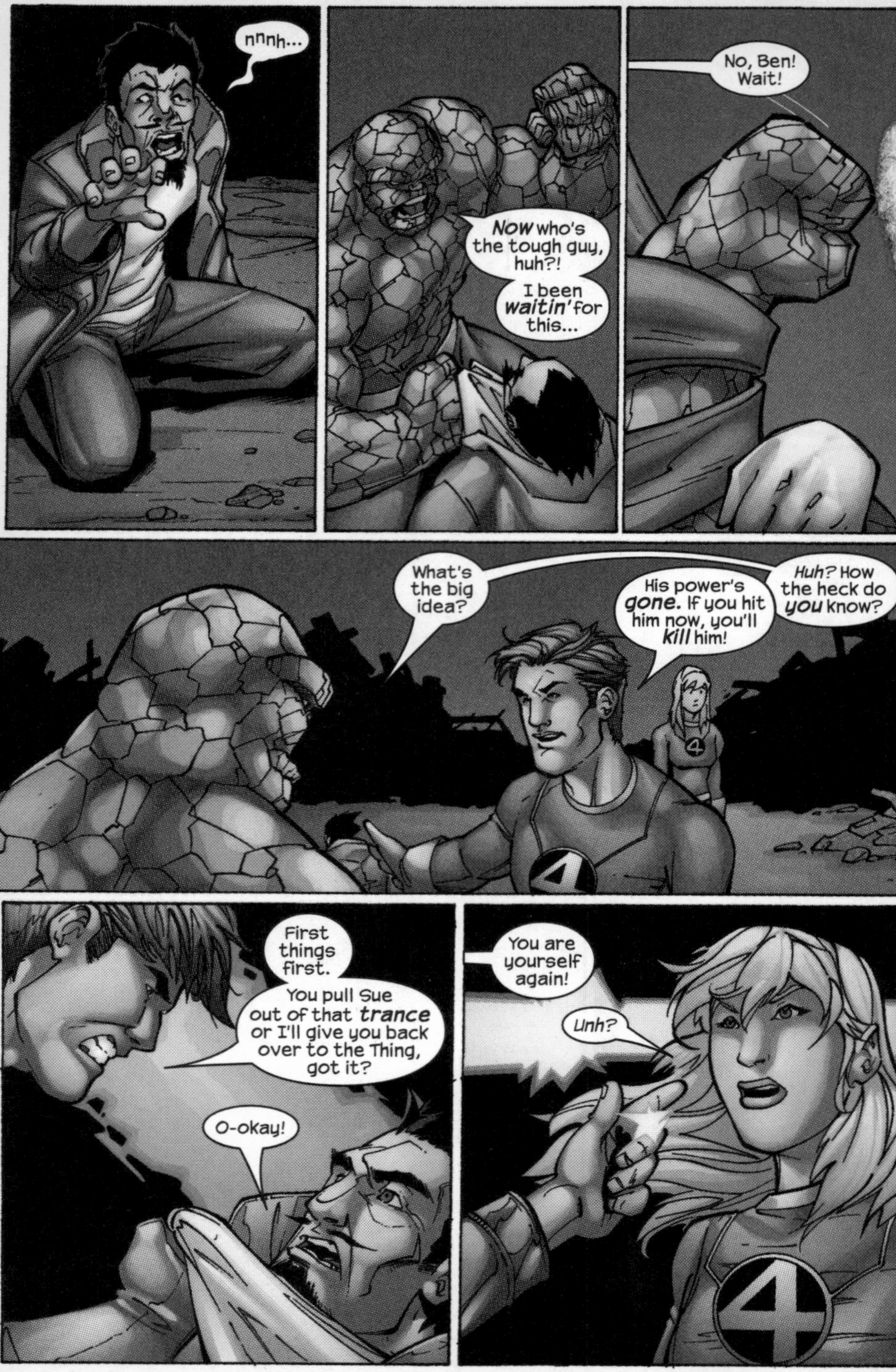
nnnh...
NOW who's the tough guy, huh?!
I been waitin' for this...
No, Ben! Wait!
What's the big idea?
Huh? How the heck do you know?
His power's gone. If you hit him now, you'll kill him!
First things first.
You pull Sue out of that trance or I'll give you back over to the Thing, got it?
O-okay!
You are yourself again!
Unh?

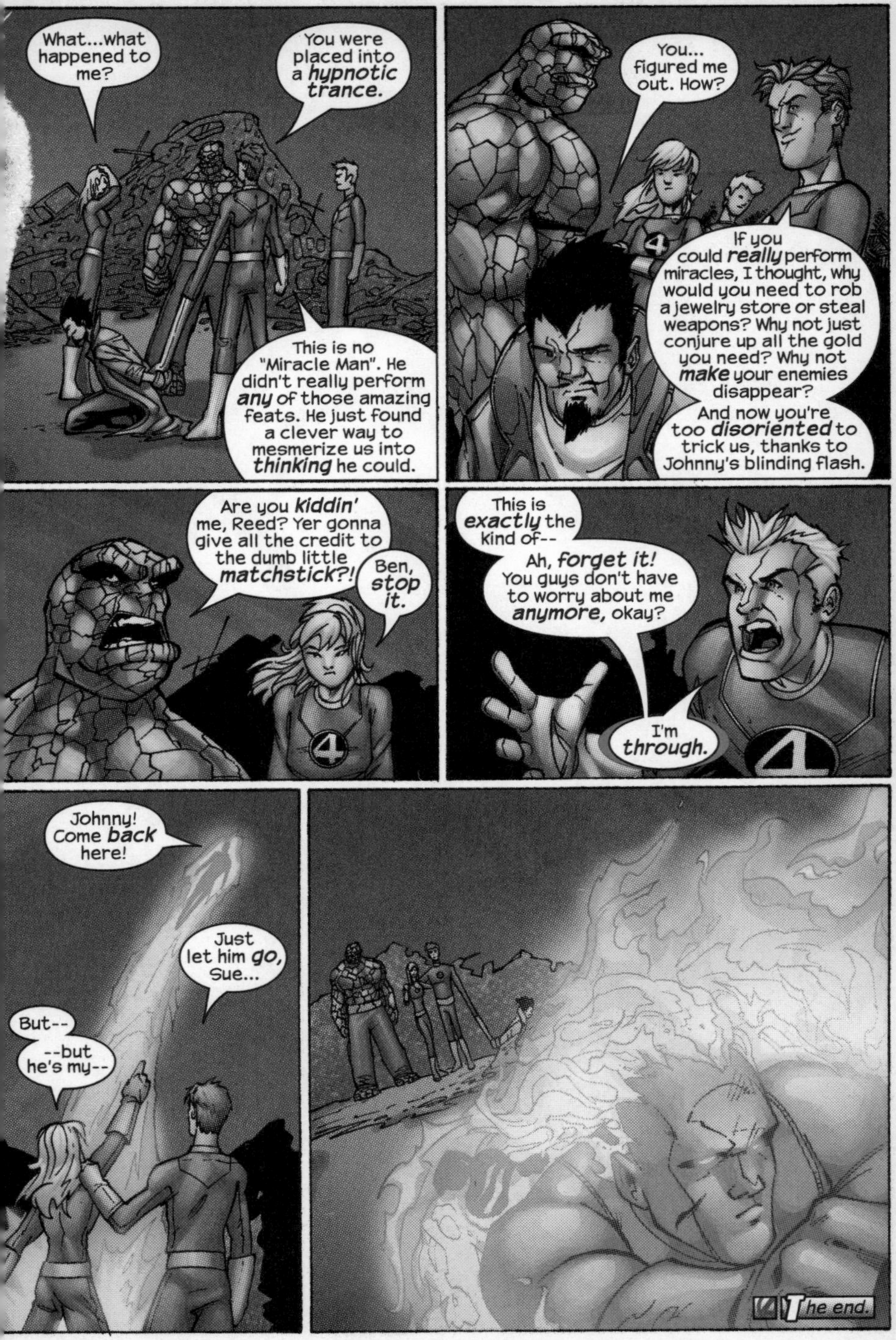
What...what happened to me?
You were placed into a hypnotic trance.
This is no "Miracle Man". He didn't really perform any of those amazing feats. He just found a clever way to mesmerize us into thinking he could.
You... figured me out. How?
If you could really perform miracles, I thought, why would you need to rob a jewelry store or steal weapons? Why not just conjure up all the gold you need? Why not make your enemies disappear?
And now you're too disoriented to trick us, thanks to Johnny's blinding flash.
Are you kiddin' me, Reed? Yer gonna give all the credit to the dumb little matchstick?!
Ben, stop it.
This is exactly the kind of--
Ah, forget it! You guys don't have to worry about me anymore, okay?
I'm through.
Johnny! Come back here!
Just let him go, Sue...
But--
--but he's my--
The end.

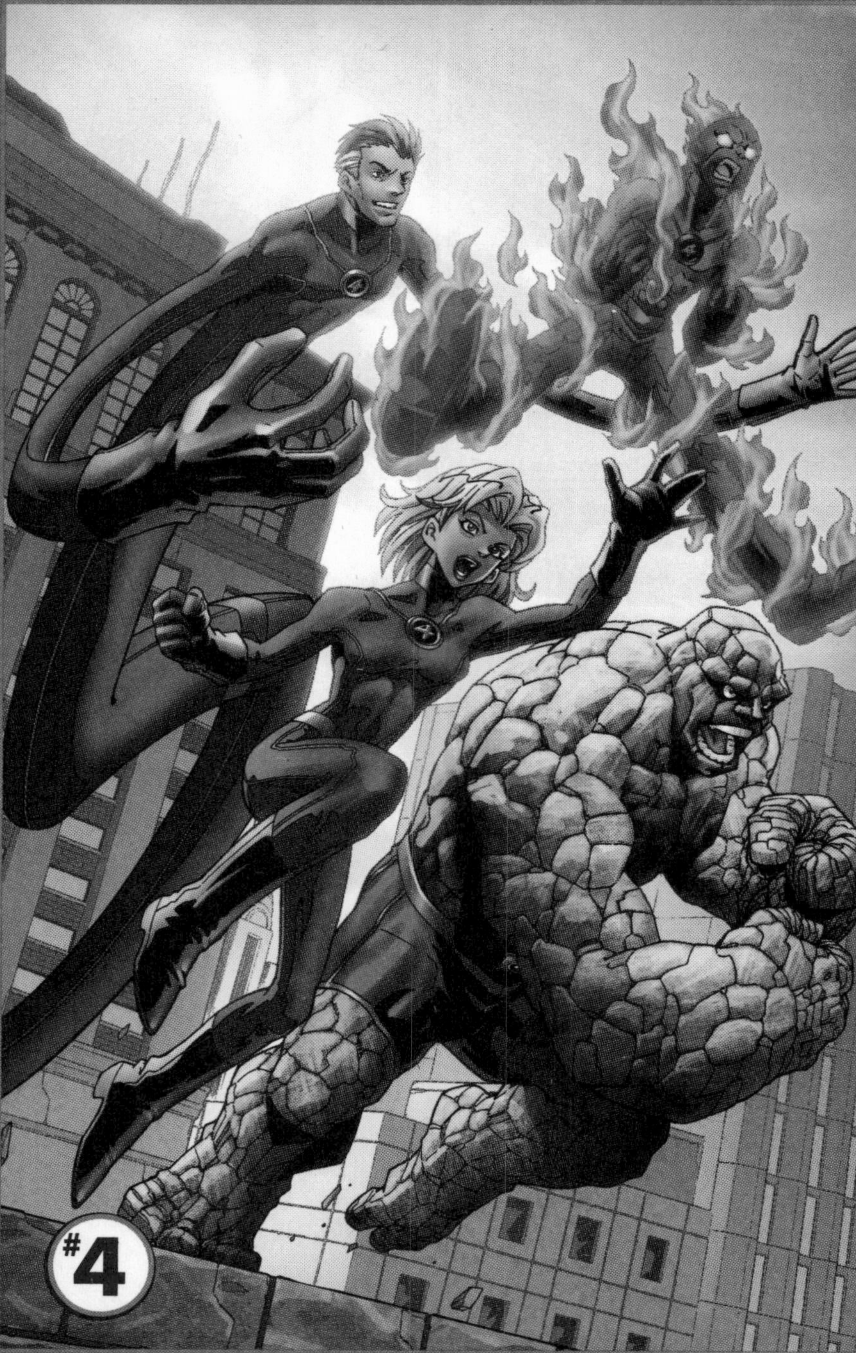
#4

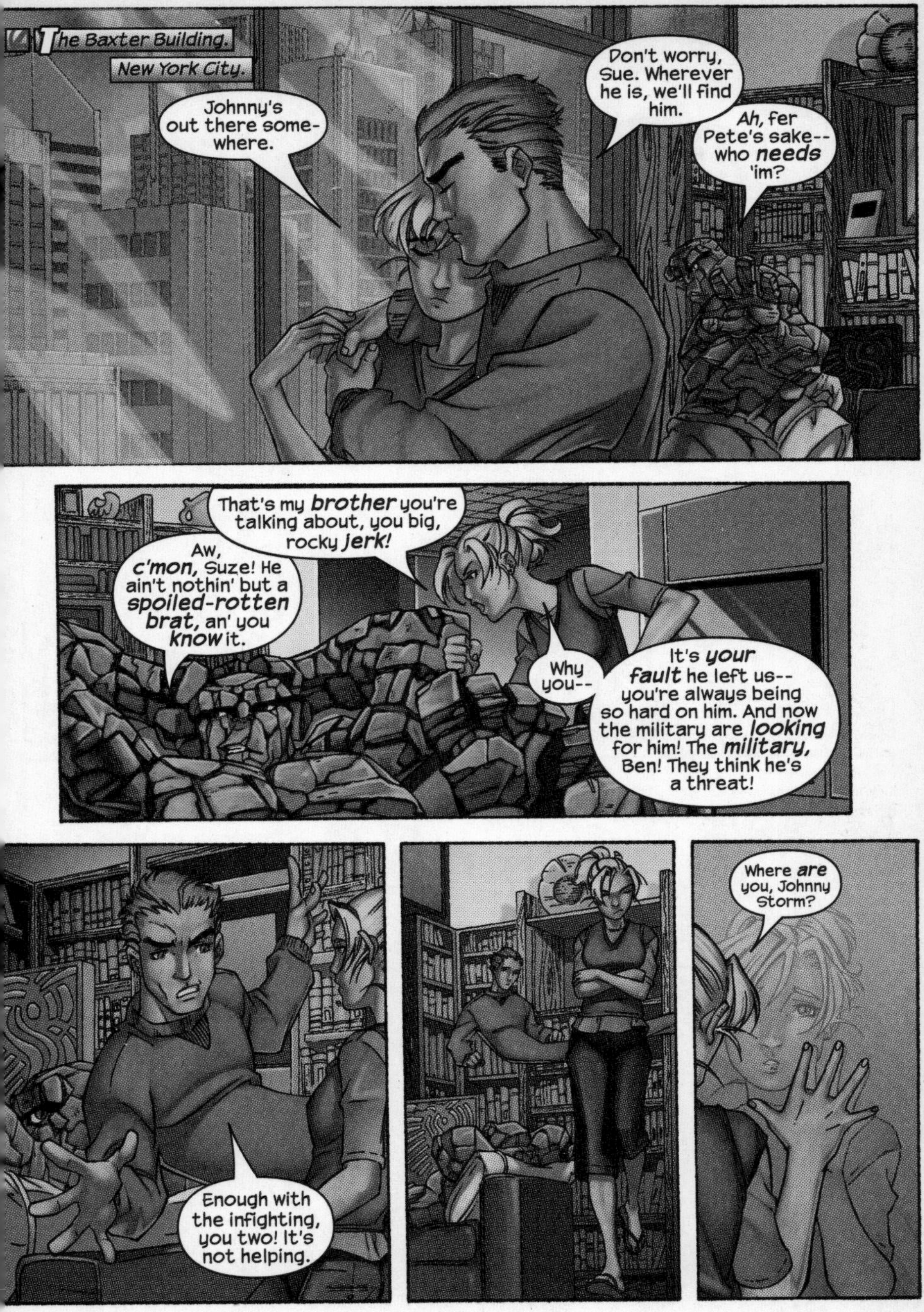
The Baxter Building.
New York City.
Johnny's out there some-where.
Don't worry, Sue. Wherever he is, we'll find him.
Ah, fer Pete's sake-- who needs 'im?
That's my brother you're talking about, you big, rocky jerk!
Aw, c'mon, Suze! He ain't nothin' but a spoiled-rotten brat, an' you know it.
Why you--
It's your fault he left us-- you're always being so hard on him. And now the military are looking for him! The military, Ben! They think he's a threat!
Enough with the infighting, you two! It's not helping.
Where are you, Johnny Storm?

Thanks.

You can come back *anytime.*

Now I remember! I know where I seen him before!

Seen who before?

The *new guy!* The one's all clean-cut. He's Johnny Storm-- --the *Human Torch!*

Yeah, right. The Human Torch lives in a *dump* like this.

Drink *another* one, Earl.

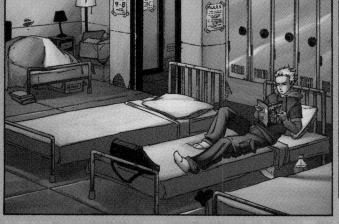

SUB-MARINER

Got into my old *comics,* did ya?

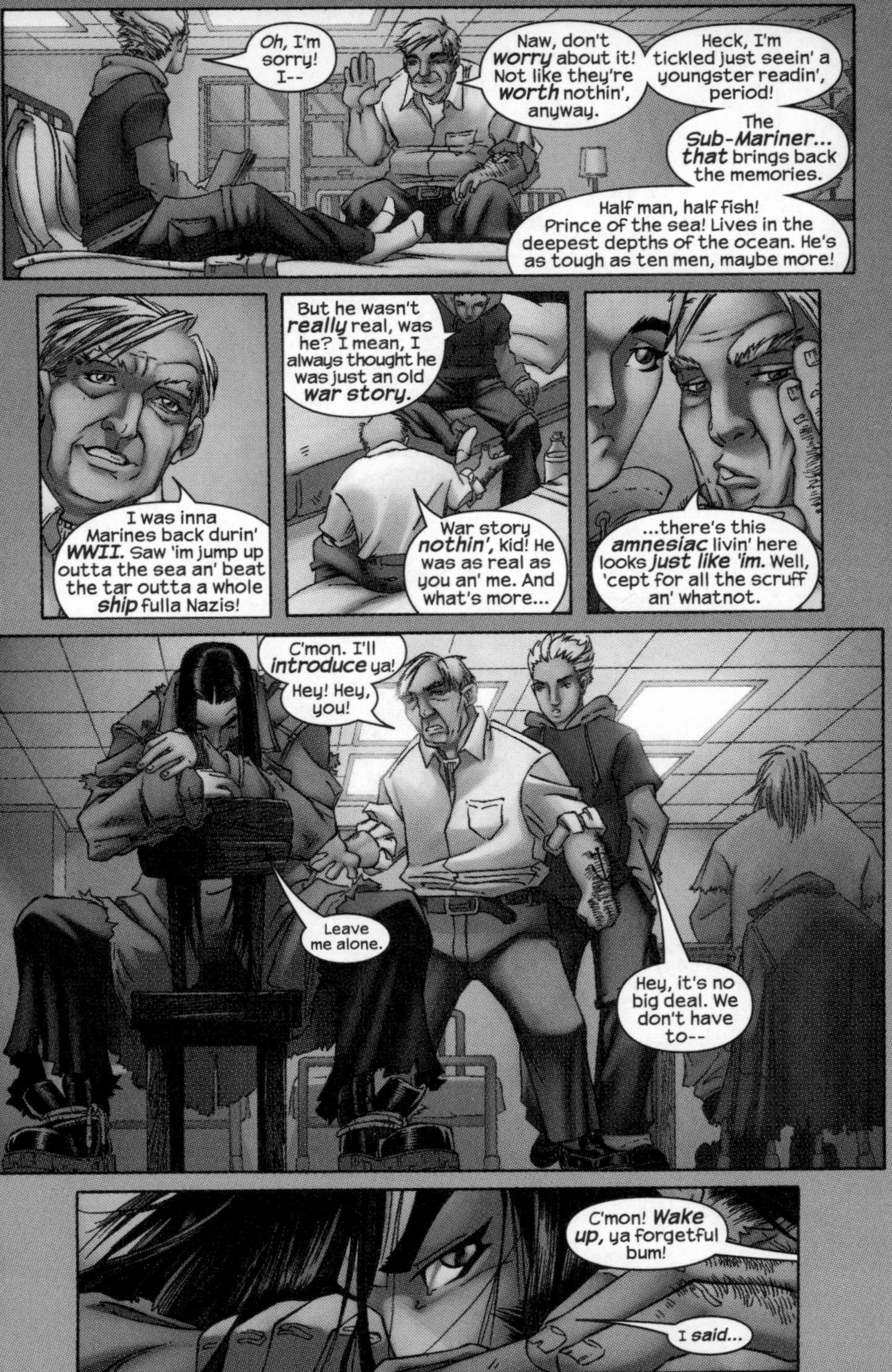
Oh, I'm sorry! I--
Naw, don't worry about it! Not like they're worth nothin', anyway.
Heck, I'm tickled just seein' a youngster readin', period!
The Sub-Mariner... that brings back the memories.
Half man, half fish! Prince of the sea! Lives in the deepest depths of the ocean. He's as tough as ten men, maybe more!
I was inna Marines back durin' WWII. Saw 'im jump up outta the sea an' beat the tar outta a whole ship fulla Nazis!
But he wasn't really real, was he? I mean, I always thought he was just an old war story.
War story nothin', kid! He was as real as you an' me. And what's more...
...there's this amnesiac livin' here looks just like 'im. Well, 'cept for all the scruff an' whatnot.
C'mon. I'll introduce ya!
Hey! Hey, you!
Leave me alone.
Hey, it's no big deal. We don't have to--
C'mon! Wake up, ya forgetful bum!
I said...

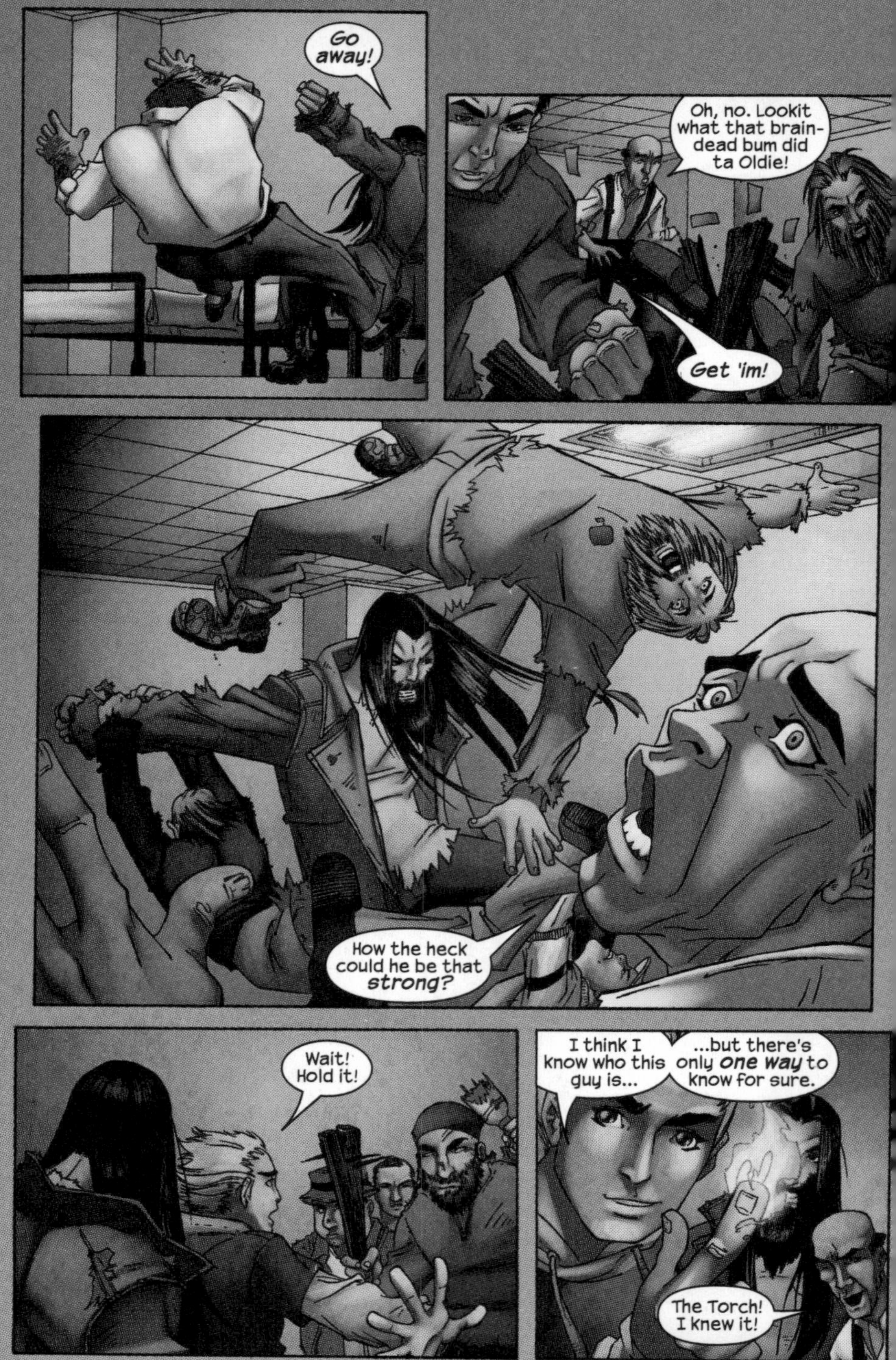
Go away!
Oh, no. Lookit what that brain-dead bum did ta Oldie!
Get 'im!
How the heck could he be that *strong*?
Wait! Hold it!
I think I know who this guy is...
...but there's only ***one way*** to know for sure.
The Torch! I knew it!

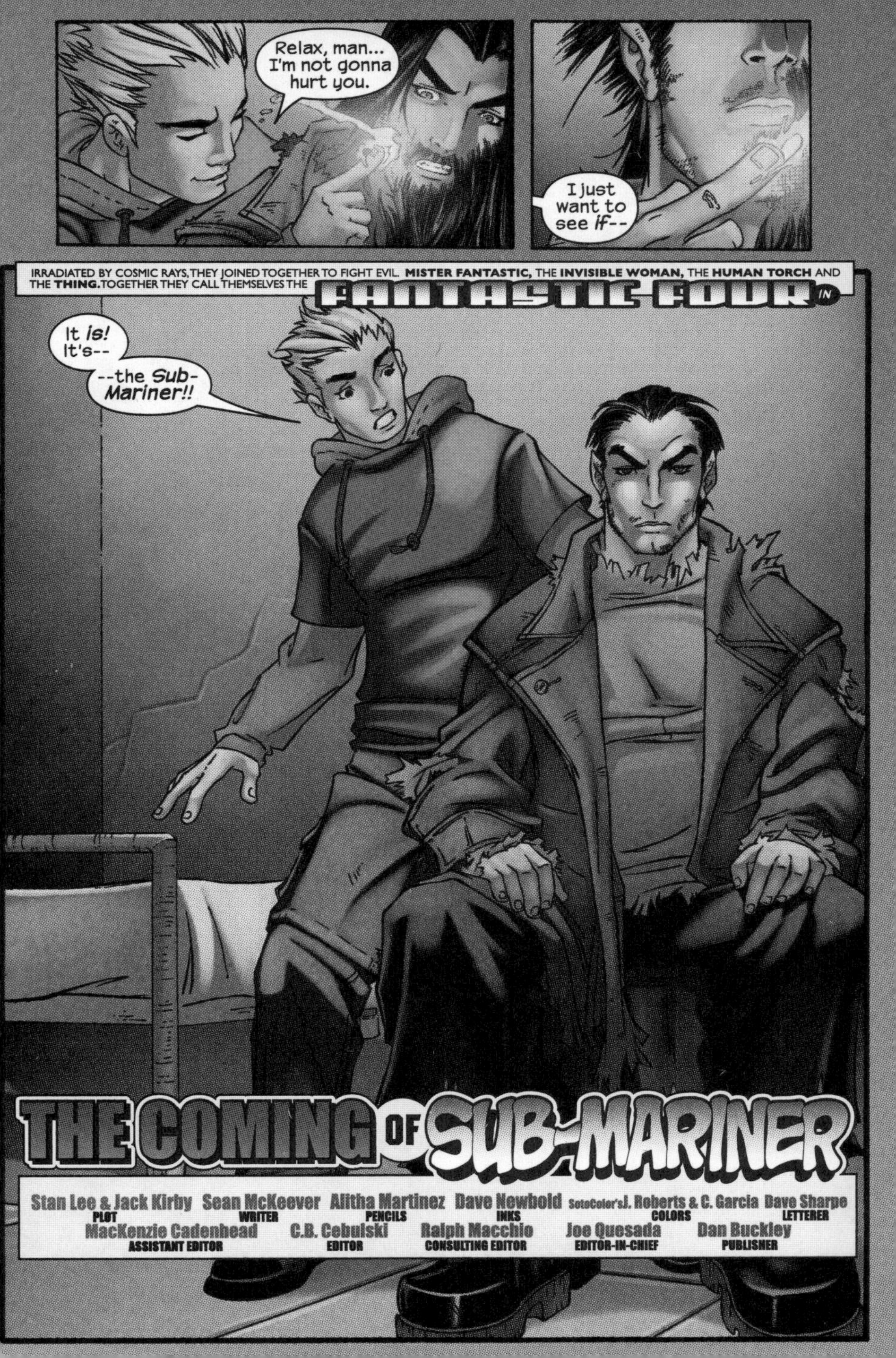

Relax, man... I'm not gonna hurt you.
I just want to see if--
IRRADIATED BY COSMIC RAYS, THEY JOINED TOGETHER TO FIGHT EVIL. MISTER FANTASTIC, THE INVISIBLE WOMAN, THE HUMAN TORCH AND THE THING. TOGETHER THEY CALL THEMSELVES THE FANTASTIC FOUR IN
It is! It's--
--the Sub-Mariner!!
THE COMING OF SUB-MARINER
Stan Lee & Jack Kirby PLOT Sean McKeever WRITER Alitha Martinez PENCILS Dave Newbold INKS SotoColor's J. Roberts & C. Garcia COLORS Dave Sharpe LETTERER
MacKenzie Cadenhead ASSISTANT EDITOR C.B. Cebulski EDITOR Ralph Macchio CONSULTING EDITOR Joe Quesada EDITOR-IN-CHIEF Dan Buckley PUBLISHER

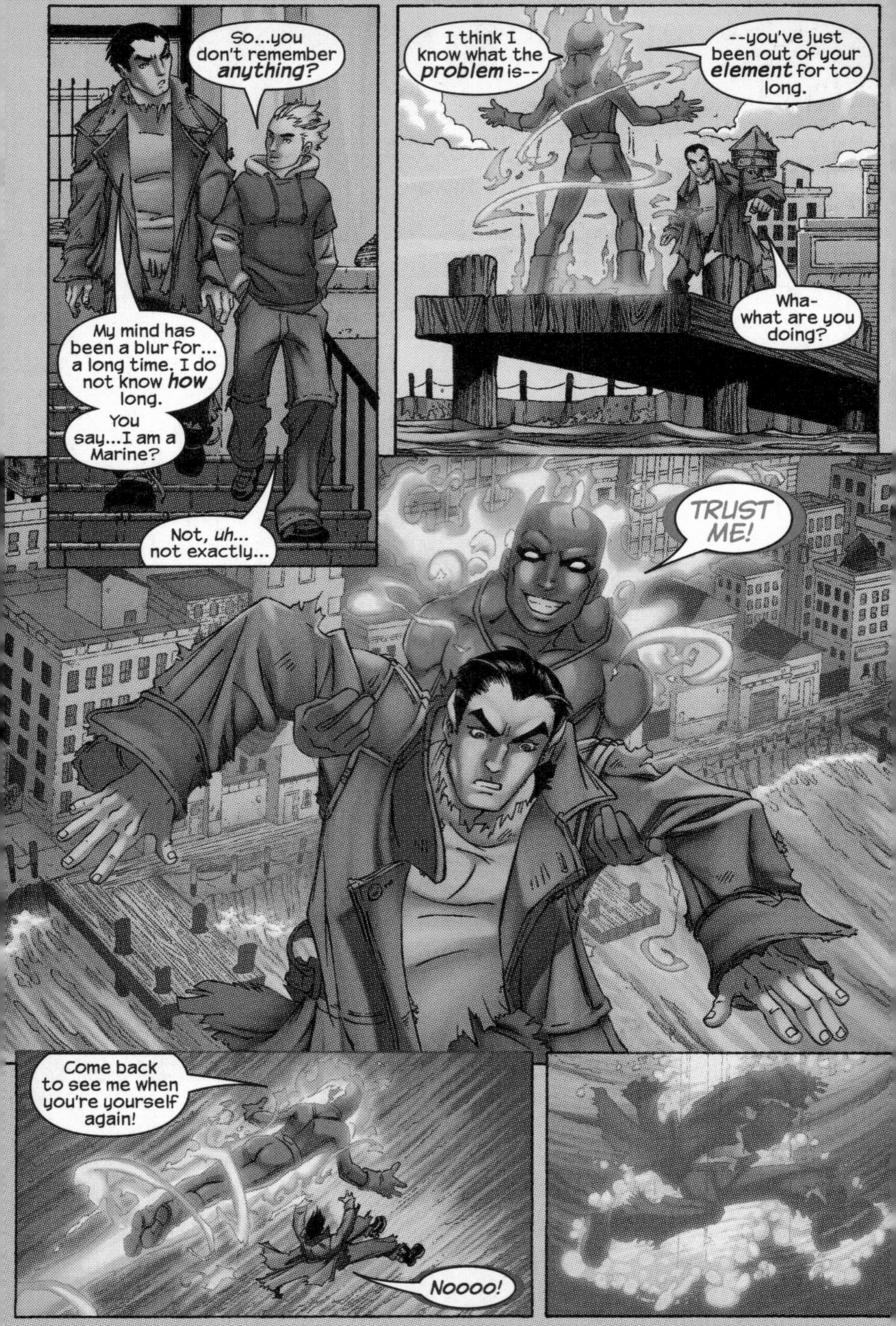

So...you don't remember *anything*?
My mind has been a blur for... a long time. I do not know *how* long.
You say...I am a Marine?
Not, *uh*... not exactly...
I think I know what the *problem* is--
--you've just been out of your *element* for too long.
Wha- what are you doing?
TRUST ME!
Come back to see me when you're yourself again!
Noooo!

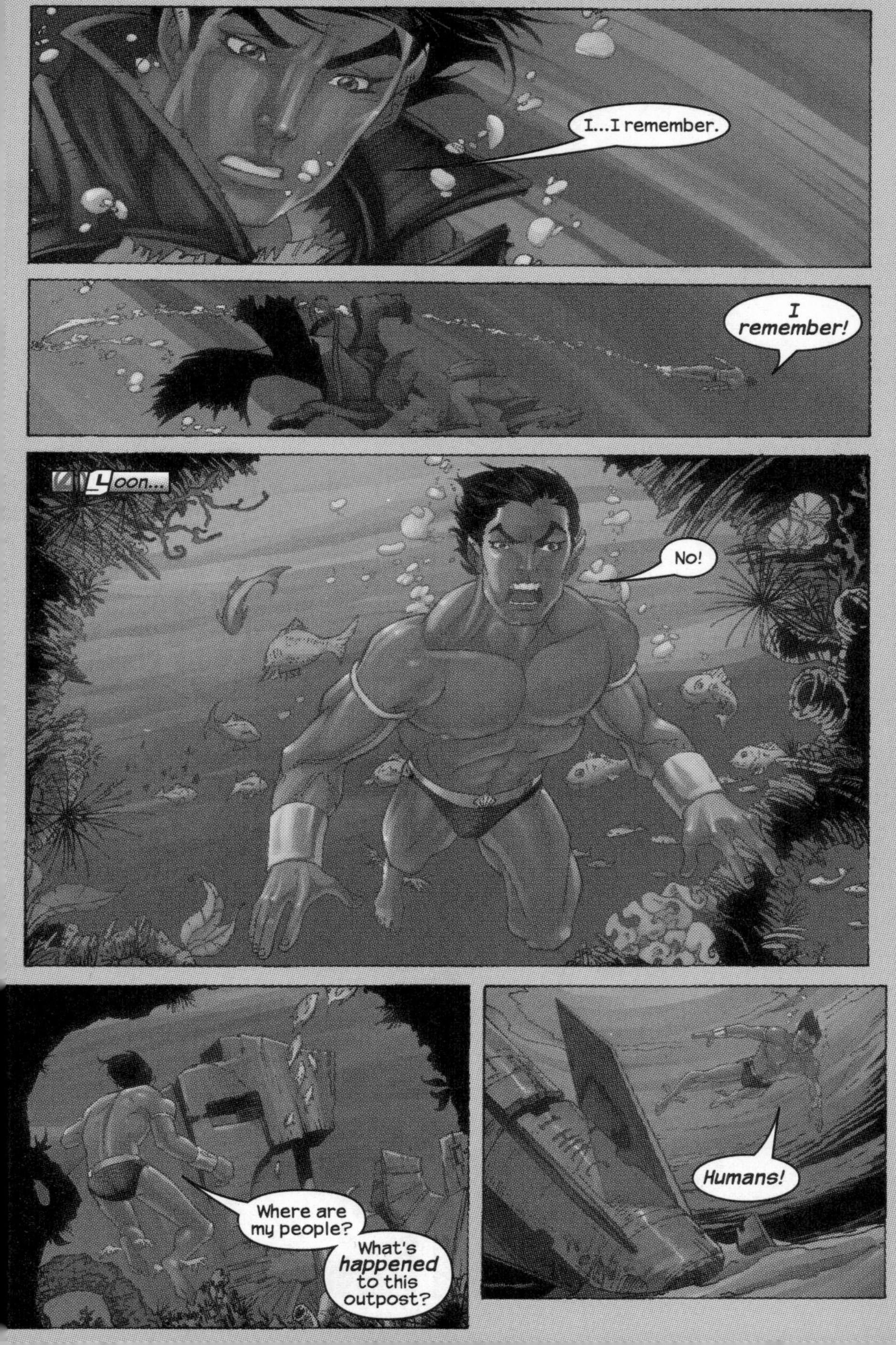
I...I remember.
I remember!
Soon...
No!
Where are my people?
What's *happened* to this outpost?
Humans!

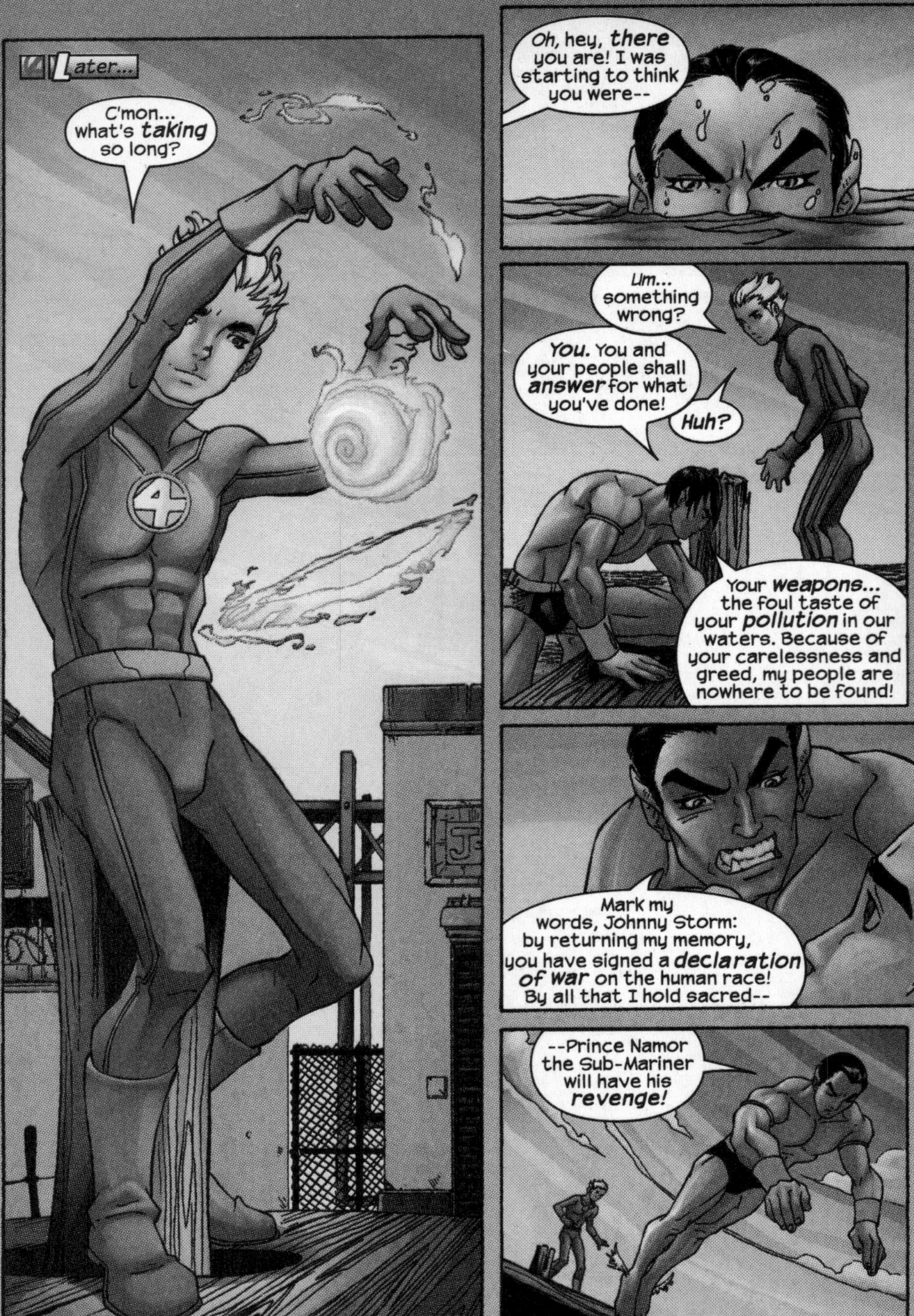
Later...
C'mon... what's taking so long?
Oh, hey, there you are! I was starting to think you were--
Um... something wrong?
You. You and your people shall answer for what you've done!
Huh?
Your weapons... the foul taste of your pollution in our waters. Because of your carelessness and greed, my people are nowhere to be found!
Mark my words, Johnny Storm: by returning my memory, you have signed a declaration of war on the human race! By all that I hold sacred--
--Prince Namor the Sub-Mariner will have his revenge!

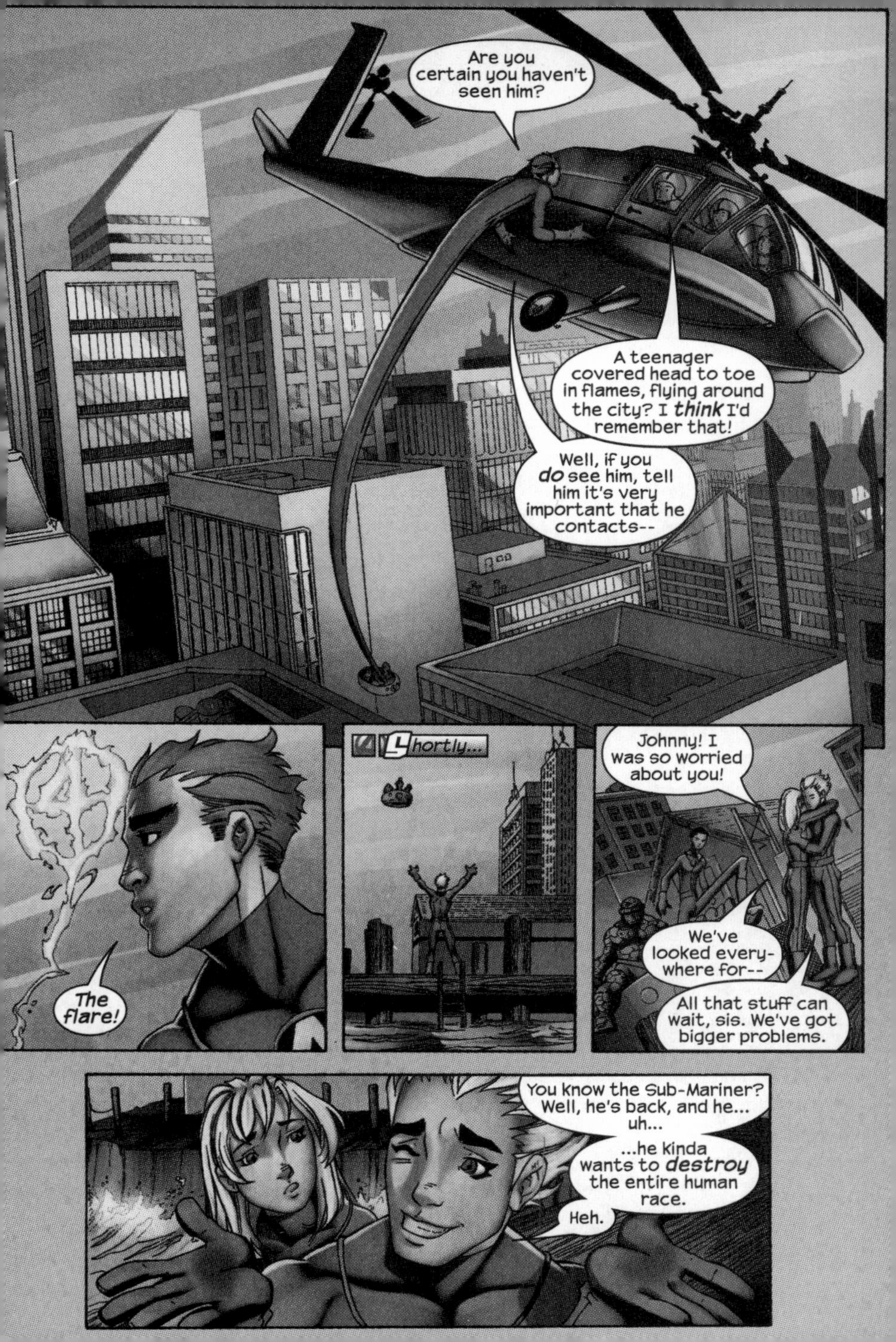
Are you certain you haven't seen him?
A teenager covered head to toe in flames, flying around the city? I *think* I'd remember that!
Well, if you *do* see him, tell him it's very important that he contacts--
The flare!
Shortly...
Johnny! I was so worried about you!
We've looked every-where for--
All that stuff can wait, sis. We've got bigger problems.
You know the Sub-Mariner? Well, he's back, and he... uh...
...he kinda wants to *destroy* the entire human race.
Heh.

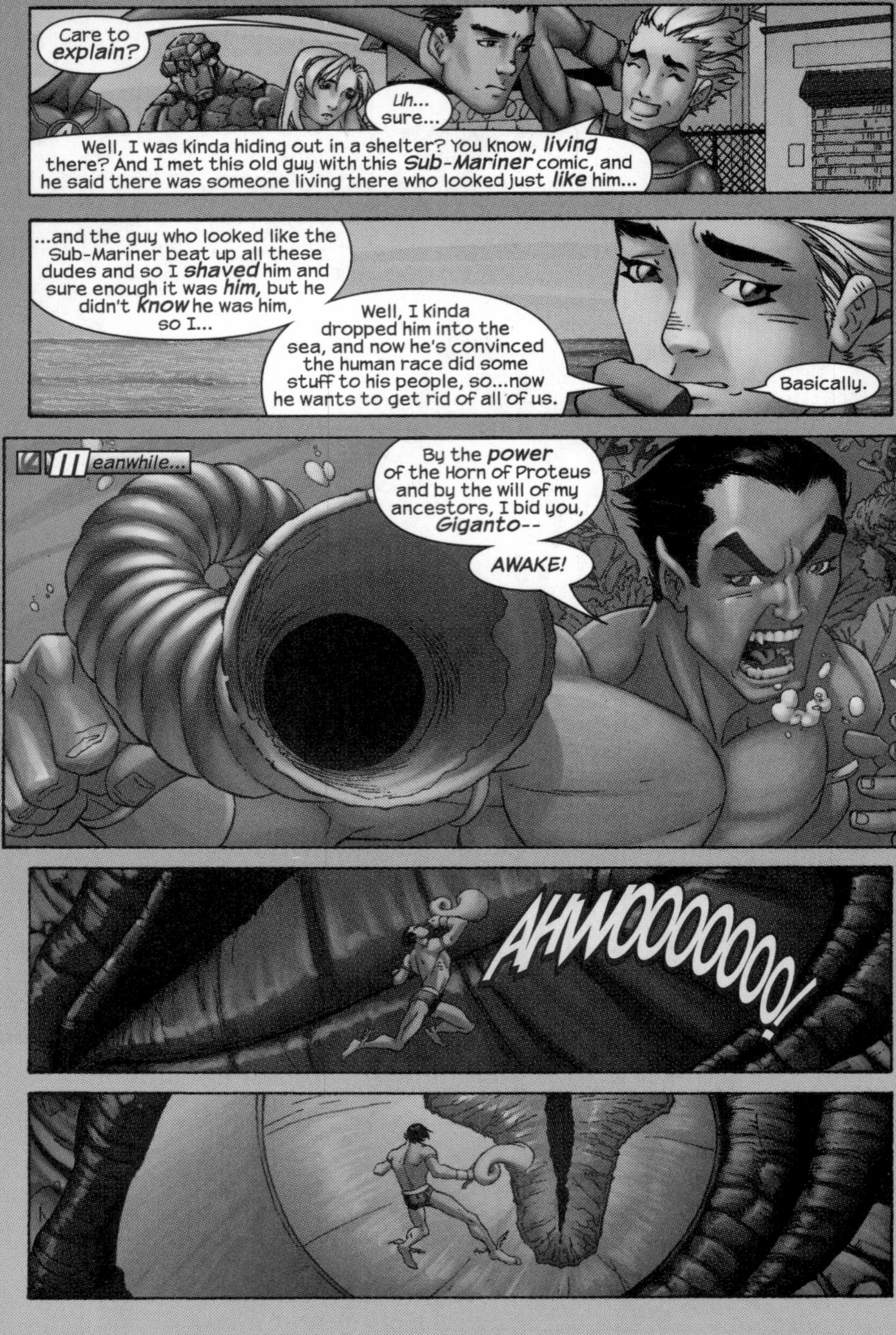
Care to explain?
Uh... sure...
Well, I was kinda hiding out in a shelter? You know, living there? And I met this old guy with this Sub-Mariner comic, and he said there was someone living there who looked just like him...
...and the guy who looked like the Sub-Mariner beat up all these dudes and so I shaved him and sure enough it was him, but he didn't know he was him, so I...
Well, I kinda dropped him into the sea, and now he's convinced the human race did some stuff to his people, so...now he wants to get rid of all of us.
Basically.
Meanwhile...
By the power of the Horn of Proteus and by the will of my ancestors, I bid you, Giganto--
AWAKE!
AHWOOOOOOO!

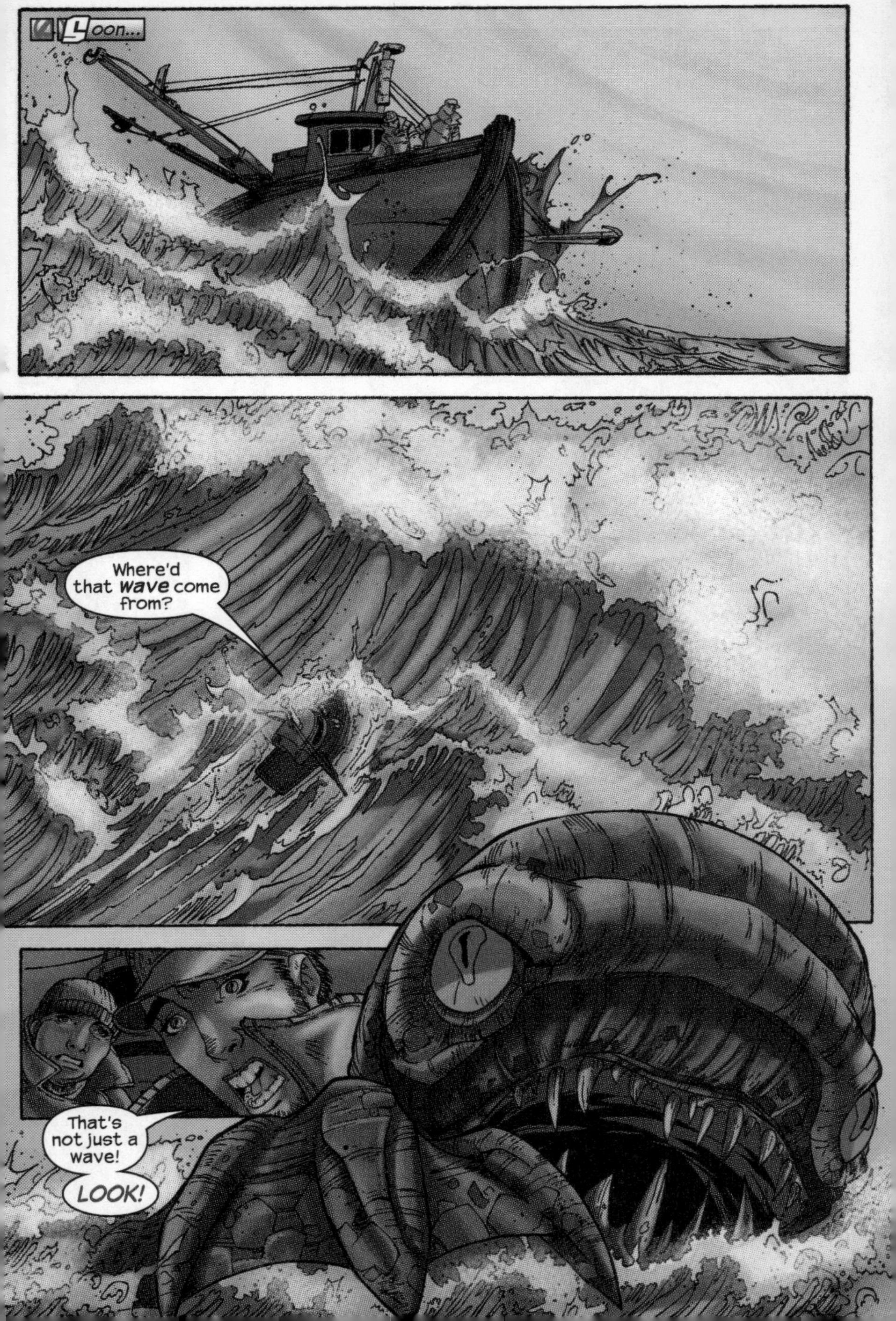
Soon...
Where'd that wave come from?
That's not just a wave!
LOOK!

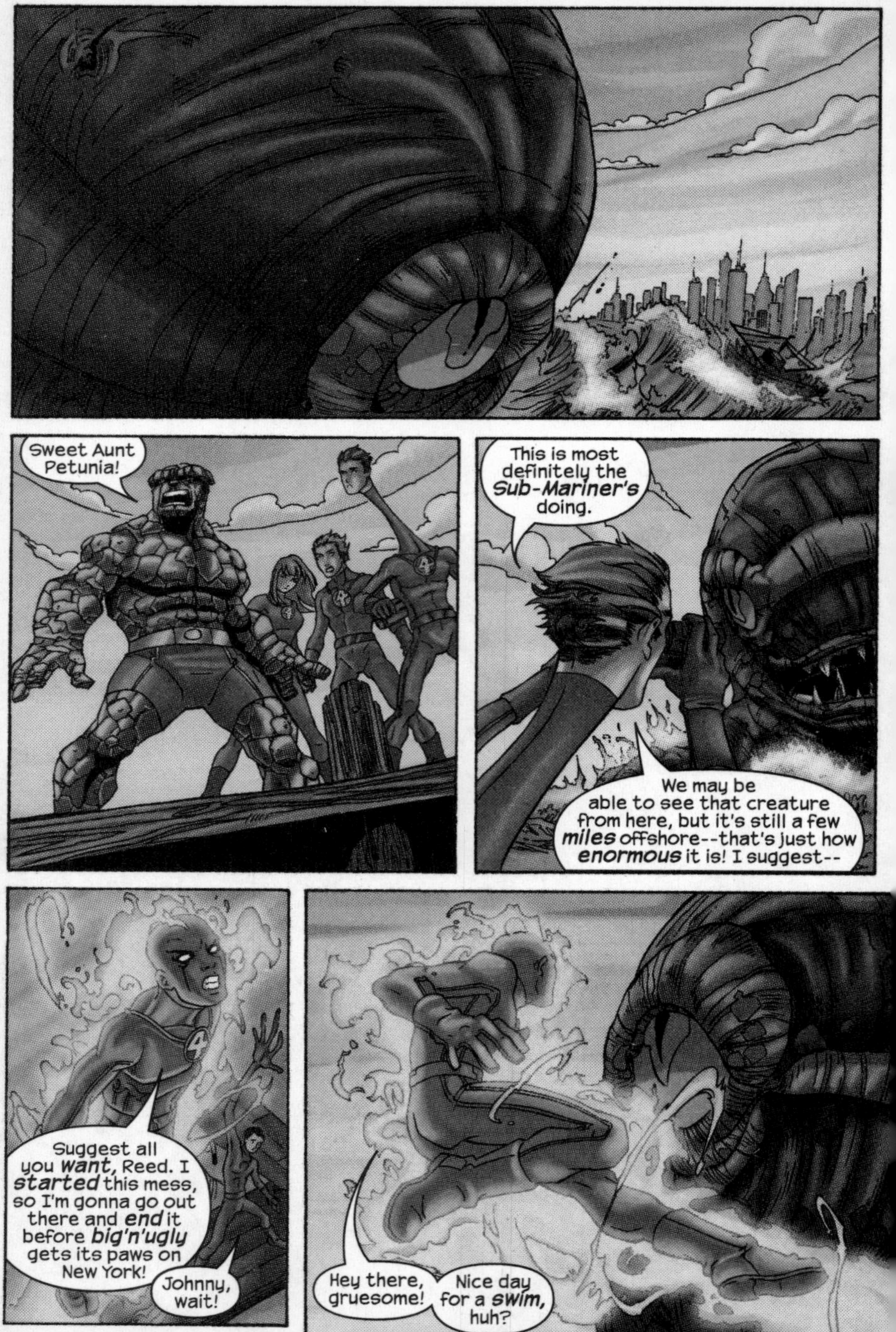
Sweet Aunt Petunia!
This is most definitely the Sub-Mariner's doing.
We may be able to see that creature from here, but it's still a few miles offshore--that's just how enormous it is! I suggest--
Suggest all you want, Reed. I started this mess, so I'm gonna go out there and end it before big'n'ugly gets its paws on New York!
Johnny, wait!
Hey there, gruesome!
Nice day for a swim, huh?

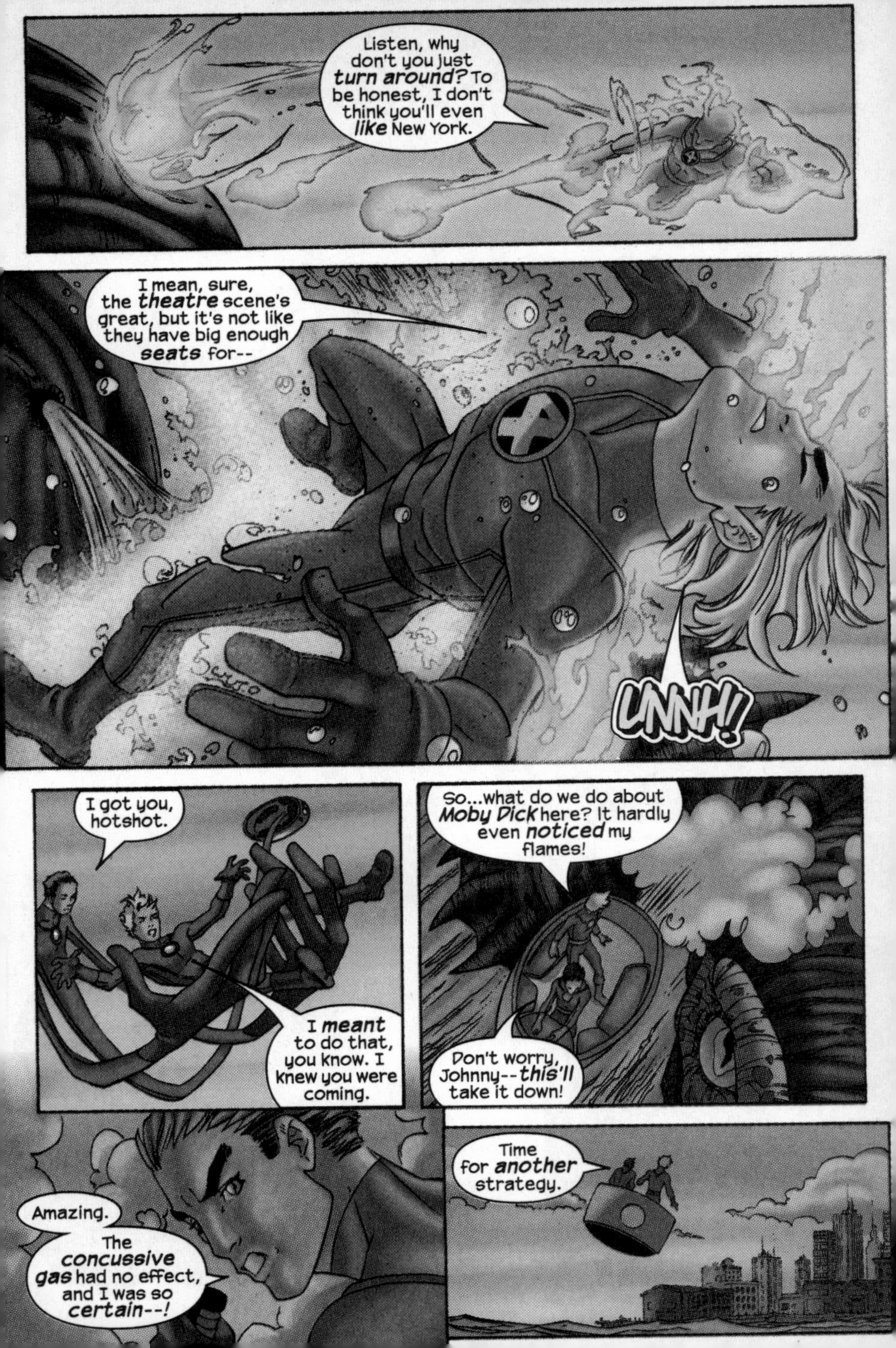
Listen, why don't you just turn around? To be honest, I don't think you'll even like New York.
I mean, sure, the theatre scene's great, but it's not like they have big enough seats for--
UNNH!!
I got you, hotshot.
I meant to do that, you know. I knew you were coming.
So...what do we do about Moby Dick here? It hardly even noticed my flames!
Don't worry, Johnny--this'll take it down!
Amazing.
The concussive gas had no effect, and I was so certain--!
Time for another strategy.

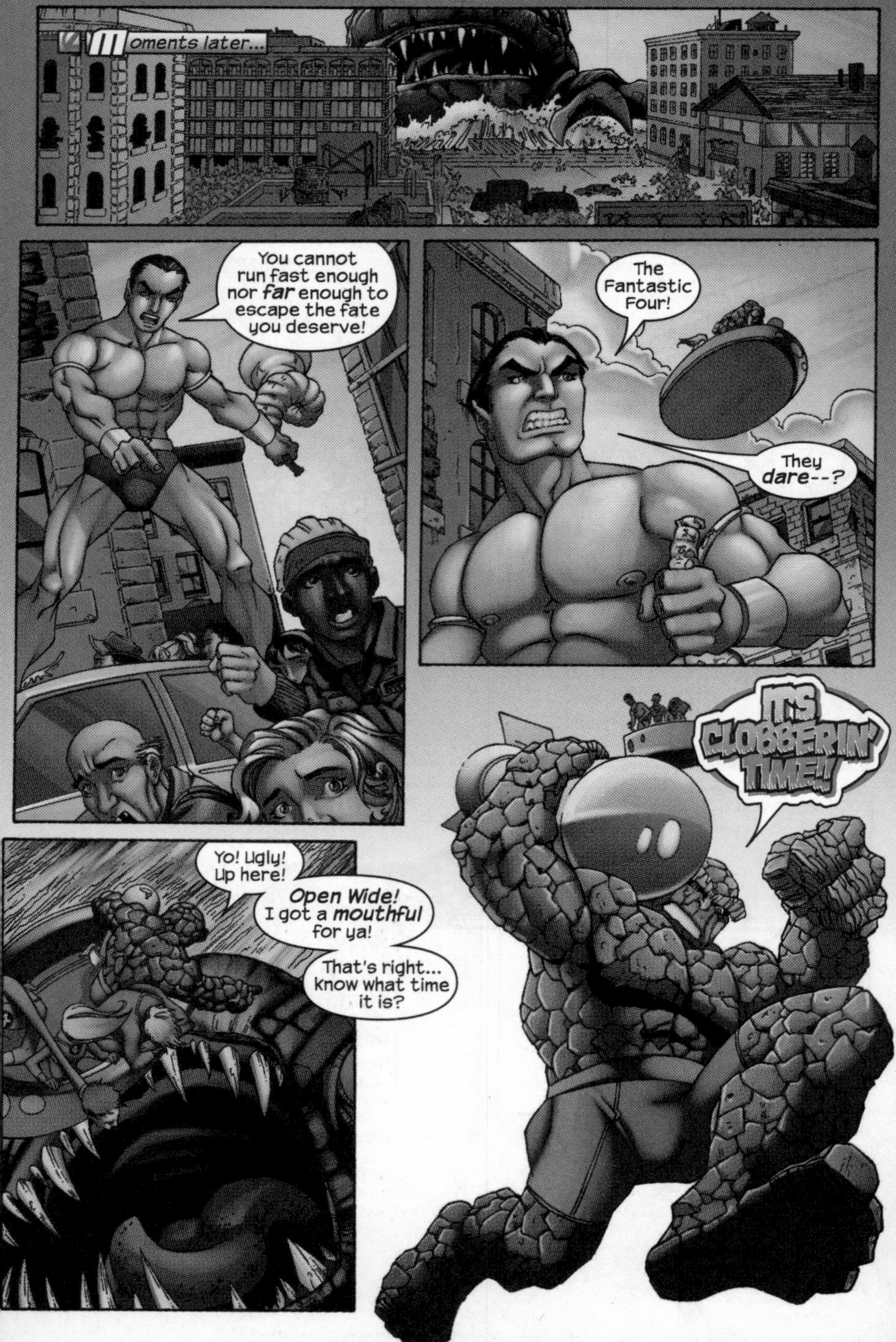
Moments later...
You cannot run fast enough nor far enough to escape the fate you deserve!
The Fantastic Four!
They dare--?
Yo! Ugly! Up here!
Open Wide! I got a mouthful for ya!
That's right... know what time it is?
IT'S CLOBBERIN' TIME!!

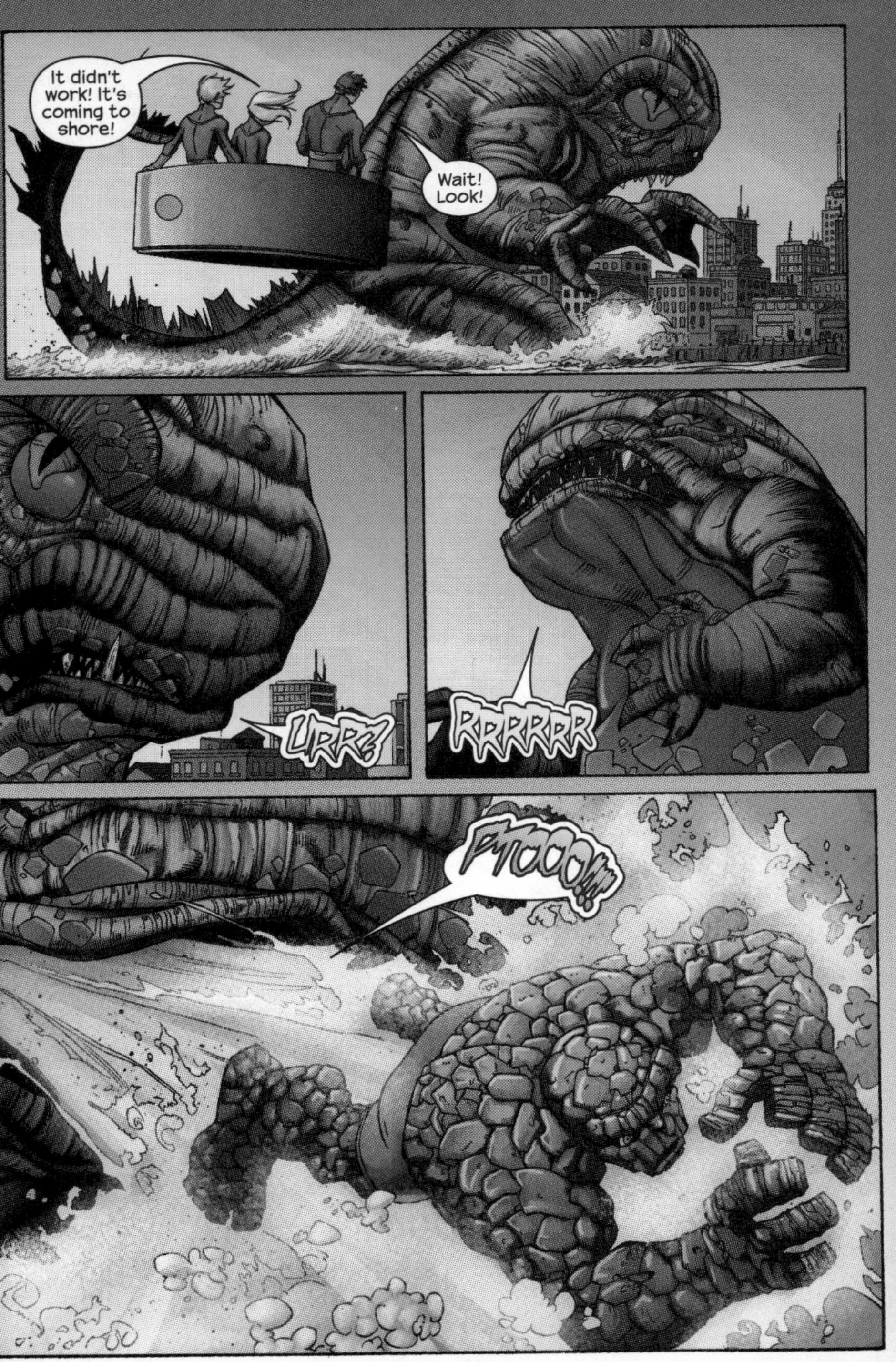
It didn't work! It's coming to shore!
Wait! Look!
URRG
RRRRRR
PTOOOM!!!

UHRRRR...

Come back! Prince Namor **commands** you!

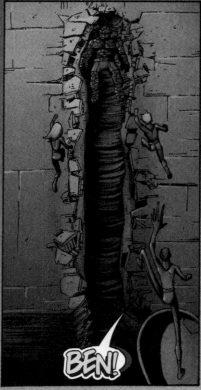

BEN!

The *indigestion bomb* I made worked! You saved the city, Ben!

Izzat so? Well, thass great. Juss lemme take a *nap* here for a day or three...

Did you truly believe the *Prince of Atlantis* would be so easily *defeated*??

Aw, fer cryin' out loud...

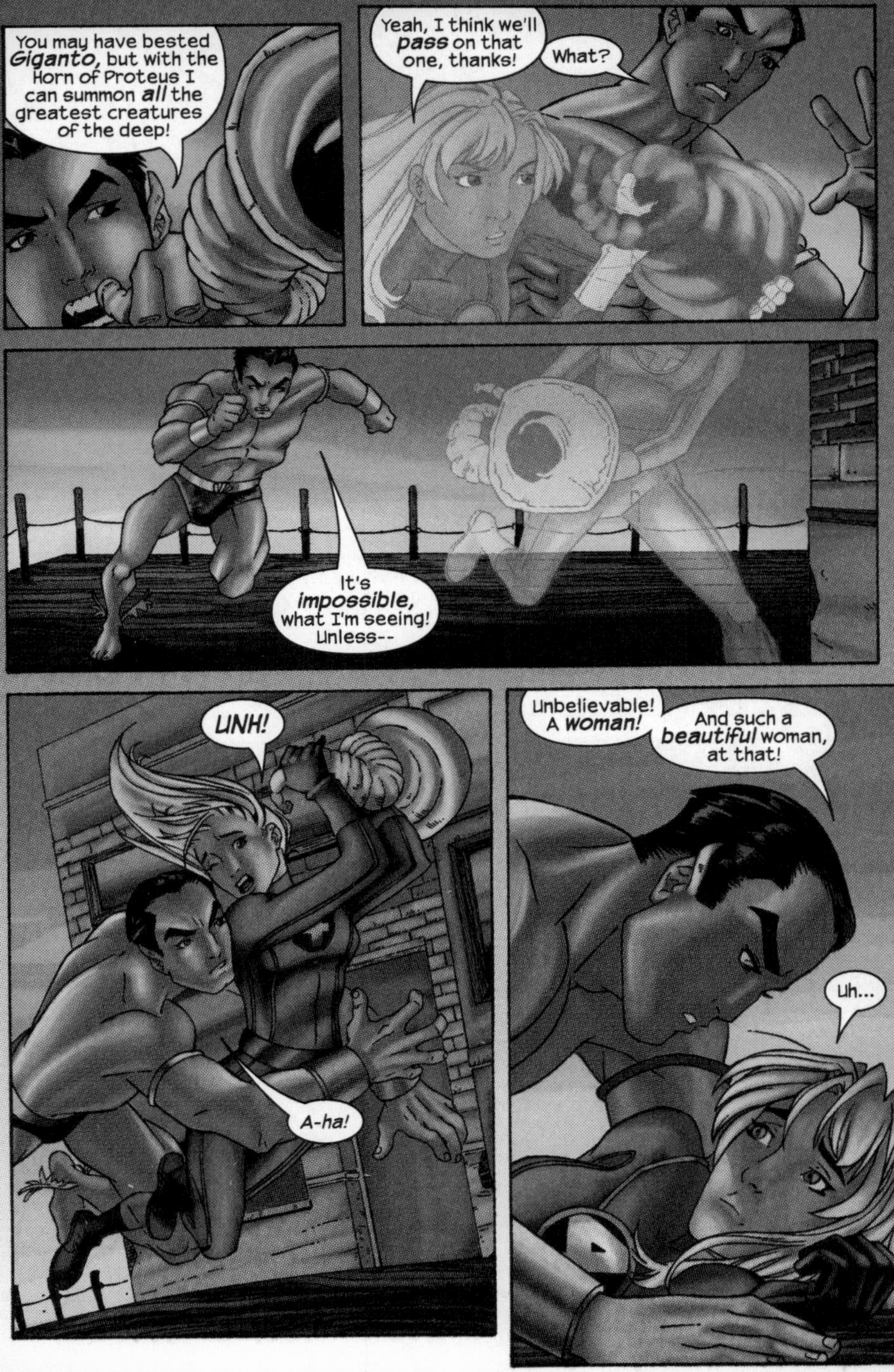
You may have bested *Giganto*, but with the Horn of Proteus I can summon *all* the greatest creatures of the deep!
Yeah, I think we'll *pass* on that one, thanks!
What?
It's *impossible*, what I'm seeing! Unless--
UNH!
A-ha!
Unbelievable! A *woman*!
And such a *beautiful* woman, at that!
Uh...

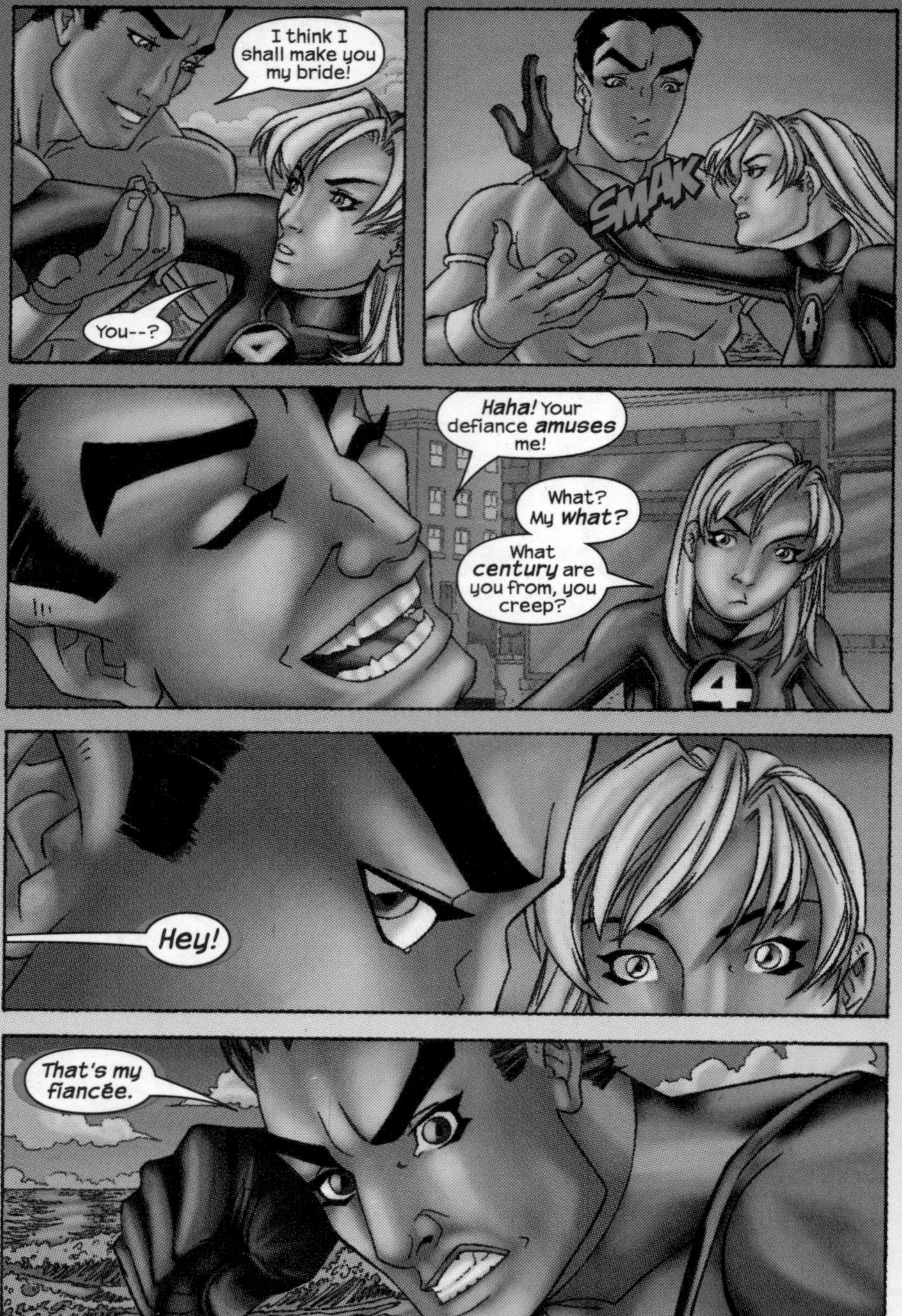
I think I shall make you my bride!
You--?
SMAK
Haha! Your defiance amuses me!
What? My what?
What century are you from, you creep?
Hey!
That's my fiancée.

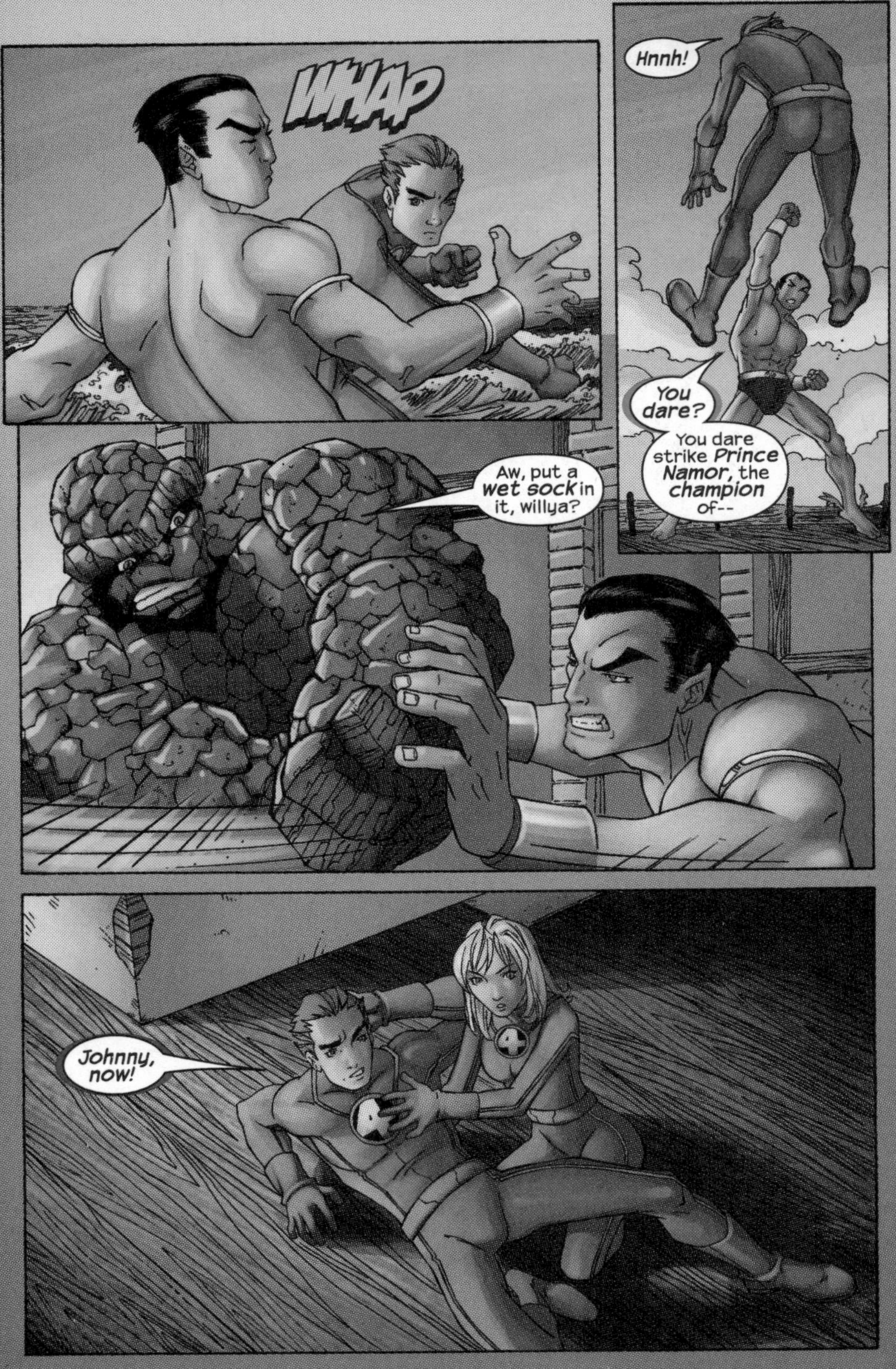

WHAP
Hnnh!
You dare?
You dare strike Prince Namor, the champion of--
Aw, put a wet sock in it, willya?
Johnny, now!

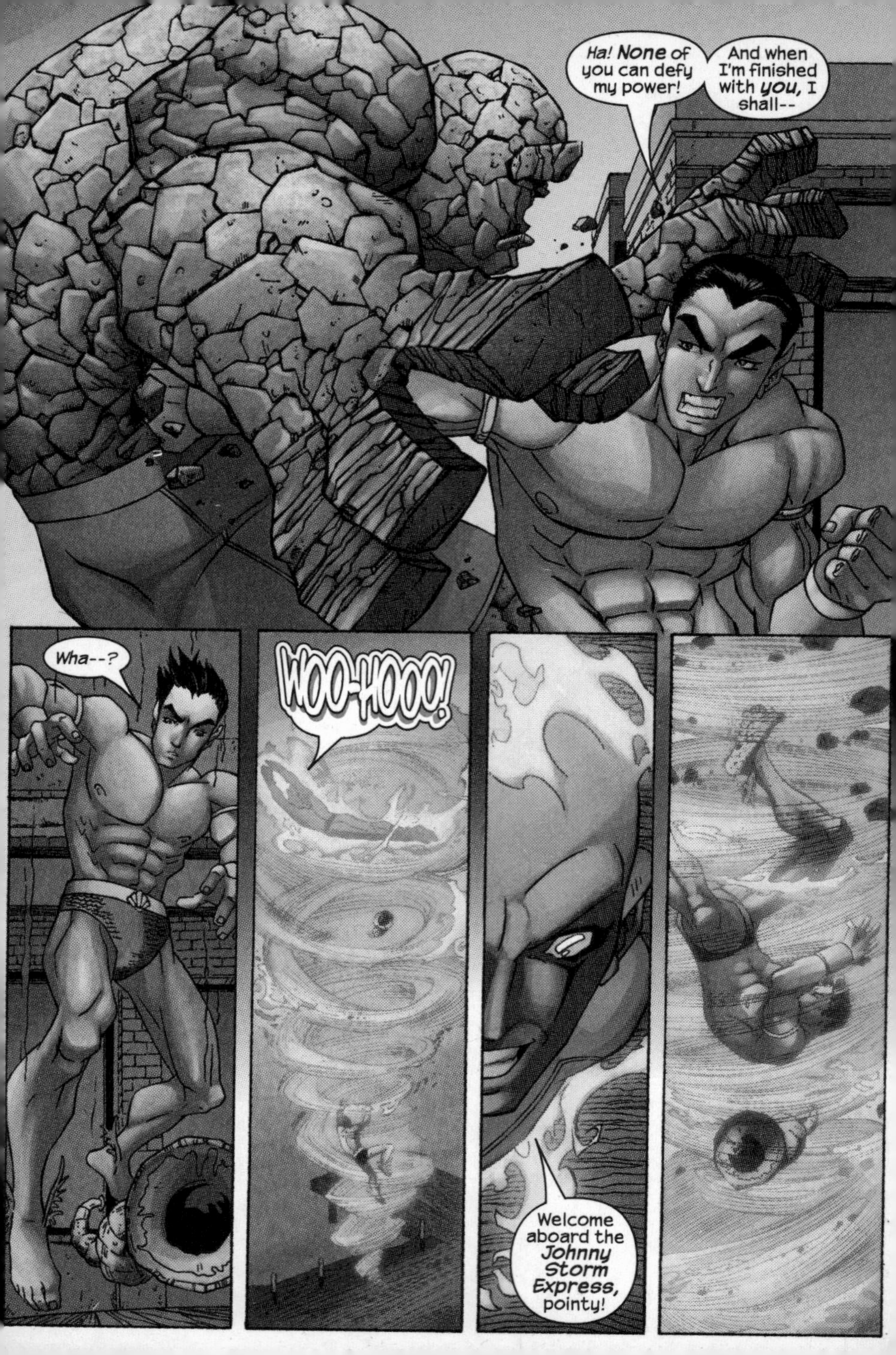

Ha! None of you can defy my power!
And when I'm finished with you, I shall--
Wha--?
WOO-HOOO!
Welcome aboard the Johnny Storm Express, pointy!

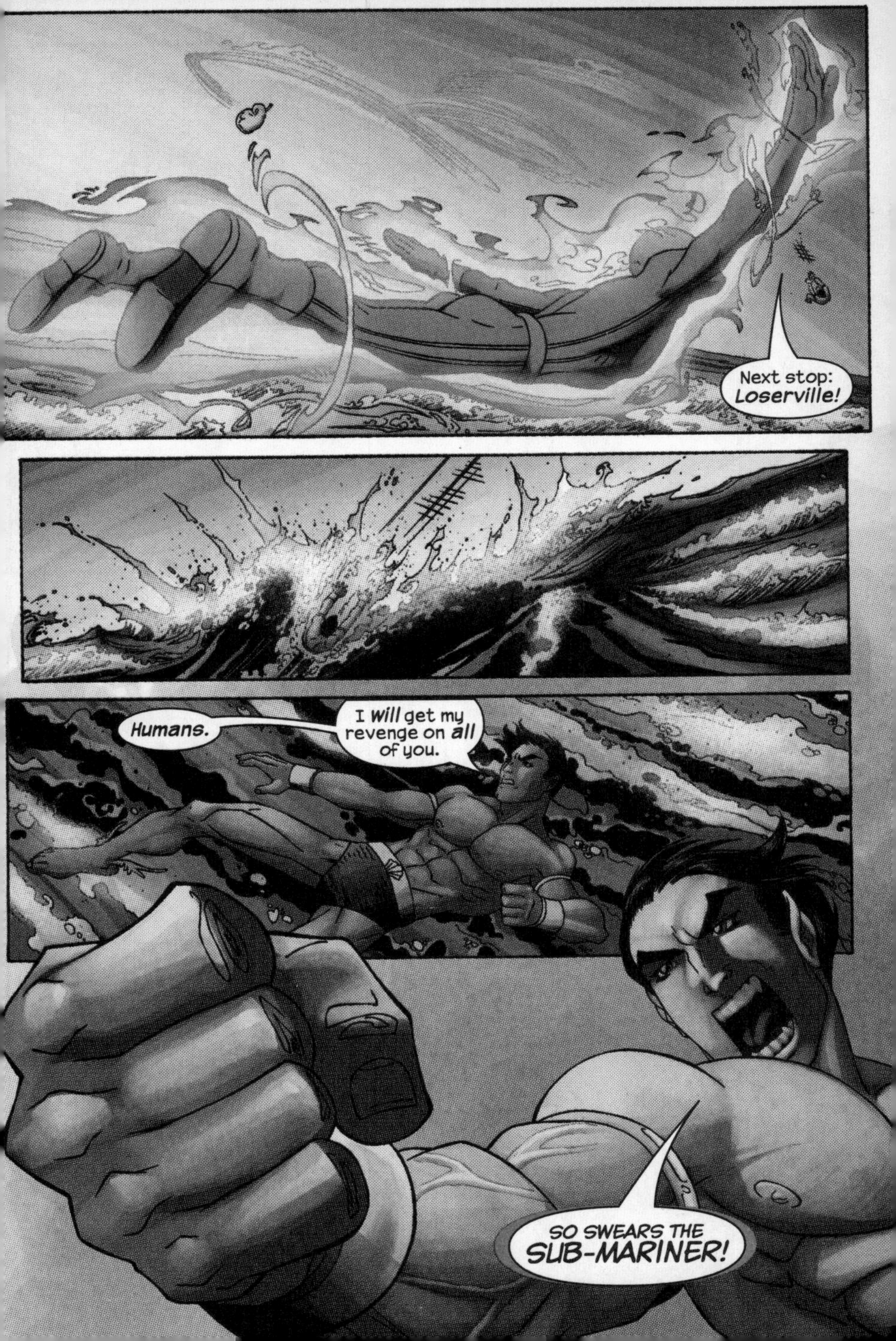
Next stop: Loserville!
Humans.
I will get my revenge on all of you.
SO SWEARS THE SUB-MARINER!

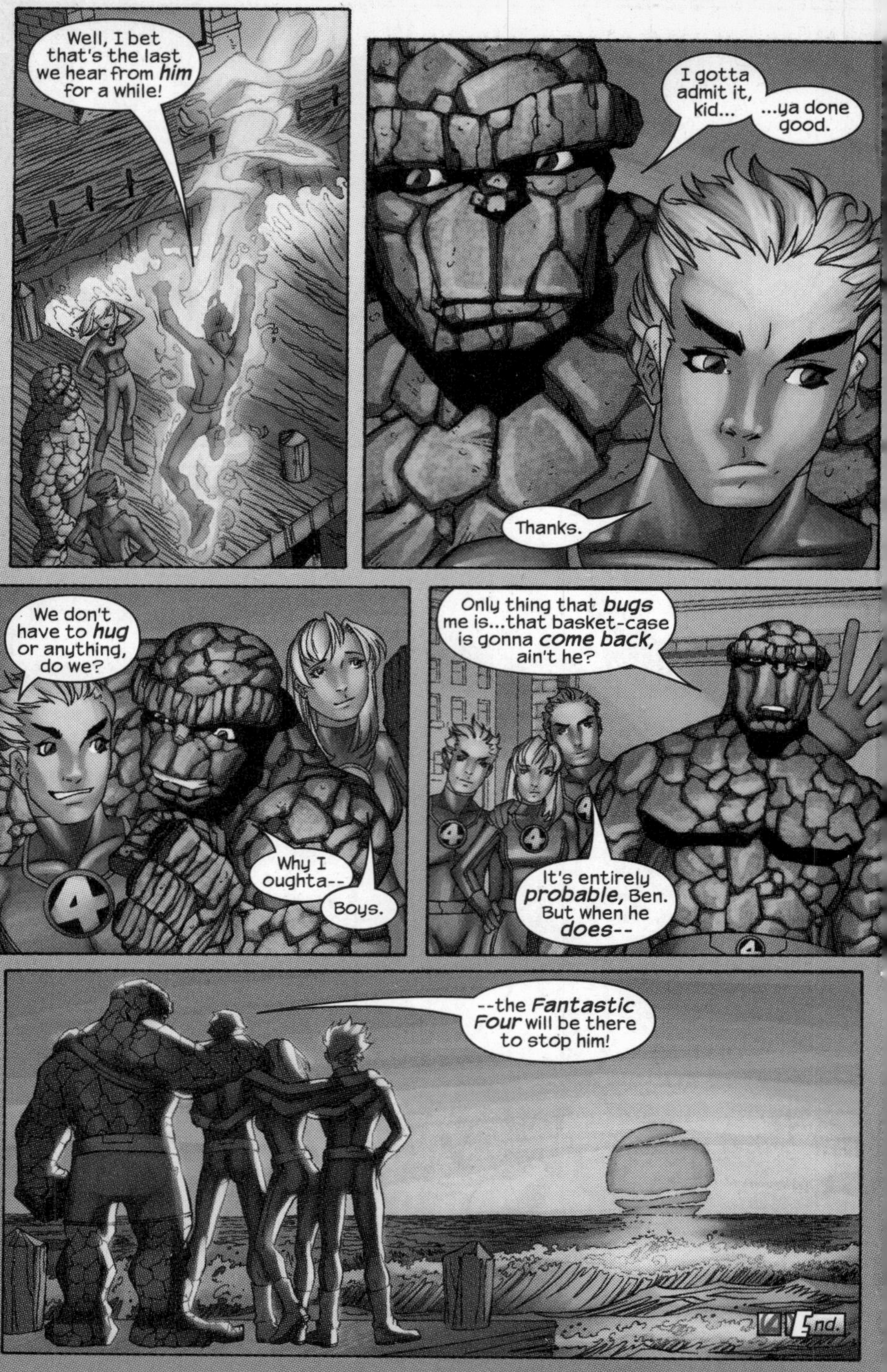
Well, I bet that's the last we hear from *him* for a while!
I gotta admit it, kid...
...ya done good.
Thanks.
We don't have to *hug* or anything, do we?
Why I oughta--
Boys.
Only thing that *bugs* me is...that basket-case is gonna *come back,* ain't he?
It's entirely *probable,* Ben. But when he *does*--
--the *Fantastic Four* will be there to stop him!
End.